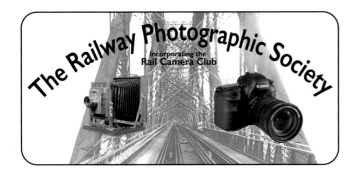

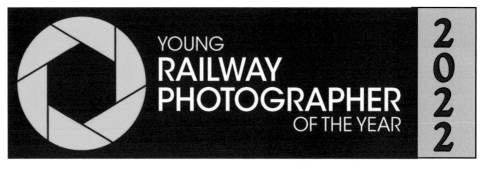

Members of the RPS photographed by Maurice Earley - seen carrying camera - in 1937 *National Railway Museum/ Science & Society Picture Library*

The Railway Photographic Society (RPS), recorded by the National Railway Museum as being instrumental in improving the standard of railway photography, was formed in 1922 by Maurice W. Earley. 'MWE' as he was often known was widely regarded as the finest railway photographer of the time and he remained as RPS Secretary until 1976 when he felt the time was right for him to 'retire'; he 'retired' the Society too!

The ethos of the RPS was to circulate prints from one member to the next in order that members could learn and receive advice from each other as by receiving comments and constructive criticism about their work their photographic standards would improve. Members had to be prepared to be thick-skinned as sometimes what they read on the return of their prints was quite pointed and vitriolic!

Over the years the RPS had, within its ranks, most of the 'great' railway photographers and each was assigned by MWE to one of the three boxes of prints being constantly circulated – the London & South Eastern Box, the Midlands and South West Box and the Northern Box. There was also an 'Inter-Circle Folio' that included pictures from the whole membership.

When MWE 'retired' the RPS some members felt that there was merit in continuing to circulate prints for comment and in 1976 the Rail Camera Club (RCC) was formed. The RCC circulated its 100th Folio in January 2018, an event celebrated with an exhibition Rail Cameramen held at Locomotion Shildon for several weeks that year.

Now, 100 years after the prestigious Railway Photographic Society was formed the RCC feels that it is the right time to celebrate this milestone of railway photographic activity by arranging this competition and to revert to its original name. On 24 February 2022 the Rail Camera Club announced that it would change its name and become the Railway Photographic Society once again and to continue with its aim to achieve high photographic standards and to record the changing railway scene.

Half title: We are pleased to start this book recording the first YRPOTY competition by reproducing a classic 'MWE' photograph. Taken at Southcote Junction, Reading, it shows the down 'Cornish Riviera' express on 23 September 1945. The train is hauled by 4-6-0 No 6000 *King George V* carrying a bell commemorating its 1927 visit to the USA. *National Railway Museum/Science & Society Picture Library*

Opposite: RCC Members photographed at Shildon in January 2018.

First published in 2022

British Library Cataloguing in Publication Data
A catalogue record for this book is available from the British Library.

ISBN 978 1 85794 603 1

Website: www.nostalgiacollection.com

Printed and bound in the Czech Republic

Silver Link Books
Mortons Media Group Limited
Media Centre
Morton Way
Horncastle
LN9 6JR
Tel/Fax: 01507 529535

email: sohara@mortons.co.uk

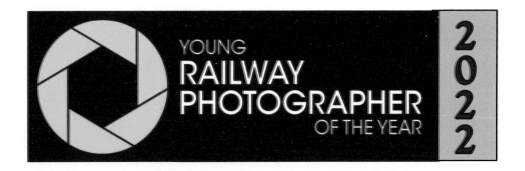

YOUNG RAILWAY PHOTOGRAPHER OF THE YEAR 2022

A selection of competition entries compiled
by John Hillier and Peter Townsend

SLP

Silver Link Books

Contents

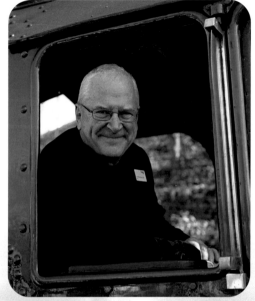

Pictures of the railway are irresistible – to enthusiasts, but also to a much wider audience. I know this, as one of the very few ways to get good news about railways into the media is with a great picture – not just of a steam train, but of any train in the British landscape.

Which is why the Rail Camera Club's initiative to run a competition to find the Young Railway Photographer of the Year is so welcome. We need young people to keep up the tradition of the RCC, and it is particularly appropriate to do this in 2022, which is the 100th anniversary of the founding by Maurice Earley of the Railway Photographic Society in 1922.

Not only is the initiative welcome, but so is the number of entries – more than 900 images, from more than 150 young people, presenting portfolios on aspects of 'the railway today'. With this level of interest, and the quality of the entries you can see here, the future of railway photography, and the enjoyment the images give to so many (including me!), is safe.

Please enjoy these great images, and as you do so please salute the young photographers, particularly the winners, the Rail Camera Club as it enters its 100th year, and the publisher, Mortons Books, who assisted the RCC with the judging, and who will make a contribution to the Railway Children charity from the sale of the book.

Sir Peter Hendy CBE
Chair
Network Rail
November 2021

Image: Andrew Lamport (see page 252)

Bradley Langton
The 2022 Young Railway Photographer

As soon as the judges saw this image (right) all agreed that it justified inclusion in the final 'run-off' between what were considered to be the best images submitted.

After having studied it in considerable detail it was clear that the image captured the true essence of the competition and was thus a worthy overall winner. Not only did it record admirably the superb restoration of London's Kings Cross terminus – and hence satisfied the infrastructure element of the theme – but it also captured the atmosphere of the fine train shed as an express was waiting to head north.

The photographer has carefully chosen a low-angle viewpoint to not only record a perfect reflection of the train and the building but also some of the essence of a modern station. True, no hordes of passengers are rushing to board their train, but had they done so the simplicity of the scene would have been lost.

It's a picture of high technical merit with some great colours and definition, which makes this a 'stand-out' shot of the railway today. The fact that it's a Class 91 at the head of the train illustrates the blend of the old and the new. Furthermore, if the viewer looks into the picture carefully many aspects of detail are uncovered and a myriad of other 'pictures' are revealed. It's a tireless image that deserves close inspection.

Full marks!

My suggestion in July 2019 that the Rail Camera Club (RCC) – of which I have been an active member now for over 20 years – should arrange a competition to find the 'Young Railway Photographer of the Year' (YRPOTY) immediately got a 'green' from RCC Secretary, David Gibson. He agreed that such a competition would be an appropriate way to recognise the 100th Anniversary of the formation, in 1922, of the RCC's 'father', the Railway Photographic Society (RPS) as well as reverting to the old name of the Society in 2022.

Having previously arranged the highly acclaimed Rail Cameramen exhibition held at Locomotion, Shildon in 2018 I was handed the task of arranging a competition to encouraging 'young' photographers who had an interest in railways. I was encouraged by the support given by RCC Members and by the competition's sponsors (see page 288) all also keen to seek out a new cohort of photographers who might well follow in the footsteps of our existing members by producing high quality images in the future which capture the changing railway scene.

We had no idea as to the level of interest that the YRPOTY would receive but with over 900 images from over 150 individual entrants, we need not have worried. Unfortunately, a small number of entrants did not follow the brief or the competition rules and could not be judged but the theme, "The Railway Seen", was attempted by most entrants although to varying degrees.

One cannot expect an entry of an 8-year-old to equal the standard of, say an older photographer although the Judges were very impressed by the high standard of work produced by those in the 'Under 19' age category.

This book contains images from every eligible entrant whose work was judged, and the work submitted made the task of the judging panel difficult. The panel, with representation from the sponsors had to consider 107 entries from the younger age category and 42 submissions from the 19-25 age group.

The pictures in this book do offer the discerning photographer some advice as what makes a good railway picture. Timing is important as is the ability to 'capture the moment'. as is skill in 'seeing' a picture and then presenting it in a way that captures interest. The judges felt that some of the pictures that were entered were too tightly cropped and hence failed to capture the 'whole' scene properly…. and that may be a learning point to emerge from a careful examination of pictures in this album that I have had the pleasure of working on with Silver Link's Peter Townsend.

John Hillier.
Barrowden, Rutland.

Having been a railway enthusiast all my life, it was not perhaps a surprise that having spent a number of years selling mass-market paperbacks I moved to the world of transport book publishing, first with Patrick Stephens Ltd and subsequently with Silver Link Publishing Ltd, having purchased the business back in 1990. For a little over 30 years I have worked on well over 500 projects, of which more than 300 have been on the subject of railways. When I was asked to be one of the judges for the Young Railway Photographer of the Year Competition and to prepare and assist in the compilation of this celebration volume, it was both an honour and a privilege. Having worked with John on four previous titles as 'his publisher', including the prestigious *Rail Cameramen* volumes, we have shared a common interest and enjoyed working together.

When we started work on this volume we were blissfully unaware of the mammoth task that lay ahead. With more than 900 images from more than 150 entrants, this was of course going to take a while! However, little did we realise just how enjoyable and surprisingly emotional this project was to be. Both John and I have experienced first hand the interest and enthusiasm that railways engender in people of all ages, be they working in the railway industry, volunteering on a heritage railway or building a model railway in the loft, spare room or garden. Photography has been an integral part in the pursuit of railways in whatever form, and there can be no greater proof of this than the entries received for this volume, which are representative of the wide spectrum of age groups partaking and the subjects being pursued.

Of course, for me having spent 70-plus years in pursuit of all things railways, and having had literally thousands of images cross my publishing desk, the most encouraging aspect of this project is to see the quality and know that the younger 'upcoming' generation's enthusiasm for all things railways is alive, well and thriving. Very good news for all of those who prefer to sit back in a comfy armchair in front of a real fire (or should that be firebox!) enjoying a jolly good railway book!

Peter Townsend
Great Addington
Northamptonshire

Compilers' note: Regrettably it has not been possible to include every one of the 900+ images submitted. In order to ensure both quality, subject balance and within reasonable retail price constraints a degree of selection has had to be applied.

Thanks...

We would like to thank Mortons Media for providing facilities for the judging. panel to consider the entries, some of which had the 'wow factor'. The judges were encouraged by the ability of some entrants to capture something very different. We hope our readers enjoy seeing the pictures as much as we did.

Thanks are due to our sponsors (see page 288) and in particular to Sir Peter Hendy. Network Rail's Chairman for finding time to personally support the Competition and to write the Forward to this book. Thanks also to Clare Irvine, his Executive Assistant. Special thanks are due to the National Railway Museum for supporting us so well and for arranging an exhibition and for hosting an Awards Evening at the Museum. We are very grateful for the help and advice that Charlotte Kingston, the NRM's Head of Interpretation and Design has given the project.

Thanks to the team at Mortons including Ian Fisher, Dan Savage and Tim Hartley; Andy Hill and Darren Hendley provided the technical back up with web design/hosting and managing the entry process. Several members of Morton's Editorial team helped (Paul Bickerdyke, Gareth Evans and Robin Jones) whilst from Bauer Media we must thank Nigel Harris, Chris Gilson and Thomas Bright. Thanks also to Pete Duncombe, Commercial Director, Jessops Europe and to the Bahamas Locomotive Society and to David Gibson and Ross Middleton from the RCC.

We spent countless hours on this book; unfortunately, there are a few gaps where we have been unable to get a response from entrants to the competition.

We hope that this will not detract from your enjoyment of the book which has almost 900 of the images entered. Finally, a big thank you to all the entrants for supporting this venture as without you there would be no competition and no pictures to admire.

December 2021

There were 107 eligible entries in this category with the youngest entrant being all of 8 years of age! The Judges were impressed with the overall standard of entries and were pleased to note the diversity of entrants. As will be seen, the images also covered a wide range of subjects, locations and rolling stock. There was a fair balance between steam, electic and diesel traction. We will leave the reader to assess the comparatives between the two age groups.

Image by Joseph Hart (see page 78)

Charlie Armstrong (14) Liversedge

I have always had an interest in trains and began to do photography over the past year, so I figured I would join the two hobbies together and photograph trains. I also joined this with my love of cycling, so have been cycling along the green way and taking pictures of trains at Low Moor station. I usually use my phone for this as it is a good camera and easy to take with me. I am also into programming, computers and problem-solving, and love to socialise with people, so I started a Twitch channel and have been streaming since January this year, making friends along the way!

Participating in the competition has allowed me to go out and look at cool railway locations and experiment with techniques such as light painting and long exposures with moving objects. I have seen a variety of stations, locomotives and carriages, and really diverse scenery of railway locations.

I have included a diverse set of stations, locomotives and environments, with diesel, diesel-electric and steam locomotives, model trains, and a mix of old and new stations. The trains are a mixture of passenger and freight trains, again mixing old and new. I have also included a mural under a station showing the incorporation of trains in everyday life.

My selection is on the theme of 'The Railway Seen', showing the diversity of scenery and locomotives used today, and the old surviving beside the new. It also shows how old stations are repurposed for other uses and how some old stations have been built upon and reused to look like the original.

Above: A painted mural under Batley station, taken on an iPhone 12 Pro. This image shows the diversity of stations and their locations in the modern day; the mural depicts everyday buildings which are the same around the station in real life.

Left: Hornby models on Batley station, lit by coloured lights and a train passing, using a long exposure with a Canon EOS 600D.

Right: A classic steam locomotive crossing Ribblehead Viaduct, taken on a Canon EOS 600D on a tripod. This image shows the amazing architecture of the viaduct, built in 1875, which is still to this day in use for many trains, including steam-hauled ones as here.

Above: A modern diesel unit leaving Ribblehead station, taken with a Canon EOS 600D on a tripod. This image shows how the old station has been restored and kept the same, while modern trains pass through.

Top right: The front of Halifax station, contrasted with the original station in the background. The image was taken on an iPhone 11. It shows that how in the modern day we have 'posh'-looking stations made of glass while the old station has been repurposed, but still looks as amazing, despite the long time gap between the years they were built.

Right: A diesel locomotive passes through Ribblehead station, taken with a Canon EOS 600D on a tripod. This image shows the contrast between the new engine and the old station.

Isaac Arrowsmith (15) Fulford (Staffs)

The photographs I have submitted excite me because they show the variety of the rolling stock that is viewable around Great Britain, and also because they remind me of the time that I first began to take an interest in photography. They show locomotives and units from all around the UK, from the North West to the Midlands to the South West.

Above: Class 47 No 47749 is seen at Bewdley during on a Diesel Gala at the Severn Valley Railway on 19 May 2019.

Top right: An unidentified Class 59 on an aggregates train passes through Somerton, Somerset, on 29 July 2019.

Right: Class 222 No 222104 makes a somewhat rare appearance on the Derby-Crewe line at Blythe Bridge due to a shortage of units on 17 December 2019.

Right: USATC 'S160' loco *Omaha* stands alongside a Class 33 diesel in the yard at Cheddleton on the Churnet Valley Railway on 25 October 2019.

Far right: Class 70 No 70805 passes through Blythe Bridge in Staffordshire on 9 February 2019.

Below: Class 33 locomotive No D6566 with a goods train at Crowcombe Heathfield on the West Somerset Railway on 31 July 2019.

John Astley (15)
Bradford

Right: No 45596 *Bahamas* is seen again rounding the curve near Damems picnic area on the K&WVR.

Left: Fowler 4F No 43924 and 'Large Prairie' No 4144 are seen near Trotsky's Bridge on the Keighley & Worth Valley Railway.

Below right: 'Large Prairie' No 4144 nears Top Field on the K&WVR.

Above: LMS 'Jubilee' No 45596 *Bahamas* at Shipley.

Liam Bailey (15) Grantham

I have loved the idea of photography in many different ways for many years – anything from breathtaking landscapes to family pets curled up in a ball to keep warm. Adding this to another hobby I enjoy – trainspotting – has led to me take many pictures of trains over the past few years, most taken with a phone camera or GoPro. The photos I take allow me to capture my emotions and feelings about the things around me. Most show my love for new, modern trains, and allow me to remember journeys and trips for years to come.

Right: Lincoln Central station is seen from the level crossing on High Street, Lincoln, on Friday 6 August 2021, with a Class 800 unit forming an LNER service at Platform 3 with a Class 158 EMR Regional service at Platform 4.

Far right: Looking from the footbridge at Nottingham station on Saturday 19 June 2021, at Platform 3 on the left is a CrossCountry Class 221, in the centre at Platform 4 is a Northern Class 158 unit, and on the right at Platform 5 a CrossCountry Class 170 unit.

Troy Baxter (15)
Skelmersdale

My photographic interests range widely, but it was originally the railways that got me into it. I got bored during Covid, so during my hour of exercise I went down to my local line, took my camera, and my passion exploded from there. Since then I've been all over the country photographing not just trains but different aspects of the railways too, as I find infrastructure just as interesting as the trains themselves.

The photos I have submitted show a range of angles of some of my favourite locations on the British railway network. From diesel to electric, from modern to ancient, from north to south, this selection of photos displays what supported Britain for years, and what will keep on supporting it for many more to come. In the Merseyrail and ELR shot, I love the angle showing various unfocused units and locos in the background as I believe this gives an insight into the depth of British railways. In the rest of the shots, I believe the angles show something unique about the railways in the UK, be it location, geography, or simply just uniqueness in itself.

The pictures show multiple units and locos, modern and new, at a range of locations, displaying what the railways have 'seen' over the years. Some are rail tours, some preserved, and some are day-to-day passenger services.

Above: Nos 50015 *Valiant*, D1501 and 144009 sit idle in the depot at Bury during the autumn Diesel Gala of 2021.

Left: No 66130 runs light through Wigan North Western.

Right: No 37800 is at the front of the Retro Cumbrian Railtour 2.0.

Top left: Unit No 777010 sits in the reverse siding at Sandhills.

Left: Nos 43010+43027 and 43192+43160 bend in and out of St Erth.

Above: Unit No 166213 leans into Kennaway Tunnel, Dawlish.

Thomas Baxter (12)
Southam

I live in rural Warwickshire and have been taking pictures since getting my first camera at the age of 3. My favourite subjects for photography include trains and railways, architecture and buildings, as well as landscapes. I have travelled across the UK, Europe and America with my camera, but some of my favourite locations are on the Settle & Carlisle railway and include Ribblehead, Dentdale and the busy Carlisle station. In the future, I would like to extend my photography to document the changing nature of the railway.

My photographs explore the heritage of railways as they develop and change. A major theme is the power of steam, the driver of the Industrial Revolution and the expansion of the rail network, the excitement of which can still be seen operating on our railways. I have also included heritage diesel traction, for a long time the backbone of power for the railways but now becoming less favoured as the railway transitions to a lower-carbon model.

The selection includes steam power in the landscape, notably on the iconic Settle & Carlisle railway. The atmosphere and excitement of steam is also shown through close-ups and abstracts. The engineering of the railway can also be seen, particularly the patterns created by points and crossovers. Finally there is a juxtaposition of steam and diesel power with overhead electrification.

By showing heritage engines and trains operating on the current railway network, the pictures celebrates the railway as it has been seen in the past, in people's memory and imagination, and how it is seen today. The direction of travel and the potential for change hints at what could be seen in the future.

Above: Tornado winding its way into Carlisle.

Right: Toot! Toot!

Taking a break.

Getting up a head of steam.

'The Dalesman', hauled by *British India Line*, crosses Arten Gill Viaduct.

An Intercity 125 thunders past resting engines, *Flying Scotsman* and *Tornado*.

Scott Beckett (15)
Skelmorlie

I only really got into photography at the end of 2019 and started rail photography around February 2020 as I was on the Caledonian Sleeper and just got hooked on everything rail. But as March came along we went into lockdown and I thought to myself that this was the perfect opportunity for me to try and get better at rail photography. I started by just photographing passing ScotRail units at my local shop as I couldn't go anywhere else, and it took off from there. Personally I think I have improved a lot since the summer of 2020, as only recently I have started to go on trips specifically for rail and general photography reasons to places such as Perth, Stirling, Glasgow, Edinburgh, Carlisle and the West Highland Line for ScotRail's 156s and 153s. What excites me about this photography series is the fantastic opportunity that I have been given to publicise my work.

In my photographs there is a variety of ScotRail stock and an Avanti West Coast 'Pendolino'. All the ScotRail photographs were taken in Wemyss Bay station, in order to try and show off the station's amazing architecture. I hope that my photos will really encourage rail and architecture enthusiasts to visit Wemyss Bay to observe this architectural masterpiece.

Above: Unit No 385027 passes Dunrod Farm, Inverkip.

Below left: No 385044 seen from the A78 at Inverkip.

Below: No 390118 in Platform 2 at Glasgow Central.

Above: No 380113 in Platform 1 at Wemyss Bay.

Above right: No 385032 in Platform 2 at Wemyss Bay.

Right: A contrast of two unit styles at Wemyss Bay.

Luke Bowerman (16)
Widnes

Above: Last of standard steam.

Top right: Postal service.

Right: Rheidol trio.

Oliver Brelsford (13) Farnborough

The railway bug had bitten me at a very early age, probably because of my Dad's passion for all things railway. Just over a year ago, after watching plenty of videos on YouTube, I decided to start my own channel. From then on I cycled up to my local station to watch interesting movements whenever I could (and whenever they appeared), and although I mainly film now, I do still enjoy photography, as it provides a level of detail and, in some ways, a lot more creativity than is ever possible with a video.

I love visiting yards and the like, which is what most of my submission is composed of; being fairly local, Eastleigh East Yard is a personal favourite and one I have visited several times this year. The station is a perfect vantage point as you can see most of the yard very well, and frequent shunting movements by a pair of Class 08s, Nos 511 and 683, means that there is never long to wait between interesting things to see. During October this year I went to Ashford for a couple of days, and on the way stopped at Tonbridge to visit the yard, which is spanned by a rather convenient footbridge. I was in heaven – there were locomotives everywhere and it was a challenge just to spot all the numbers! I have a YouTube channel and mainly do videography, but it was

a fun challenge to improve my photography for the competition.

I try to take my photographs from different angles, from bridges, platforms and lineside paths. I have tried to reflect how the railway is seen 'as is', and to reflect the variety of current rolling stock, old and new.

Left: This short line of four GBRf locomotives stabled at Tonbridge West Yard on 24 October 2021 features no fewer than three 'celebrities' – from the extreme left, No 73201 *Broadlands*, then Nos 69002 *Bob Tiller CM&EE*, 69001 *Mayflower*, 73963 *Janice* and 66793.

Right: My Dad mentioned an old TV advert for the original Minis, with the slogan 'Minis have feelings too!', an ideal caption for two Class 444 units, Nos 444008 and 444019, coupled together at Basingstoke on 20 June 2021 forming a service for London Waterloo.

Above: Ready for action: Nos 66144 and 66846 await their next turns in Eastleigh East Yard on 20 June 2021. I felt this picture was framed very well and portrays the locomotives as the mighty workhorses they are.

Thomas Briggs (15)
North Shields

Right: A TransPennine Express Class 350 stands at Edinburgh Waverley waiting to depart for Manchester Airport while a ScotRail Class 380 waits to depart to Glasgow Central.

Below: Two DRS Class 68s fly through Morpeth station heading north towards Scotland.

Below right: The new TransPennine Express Class 802 IEP sits at Newcastle on a test movement between Newcastle and York.

YOUNG
**RAILWAY
PHOTOGRAPHER**
OF THE YEAR

Under 19 portfolio: Rowan Harris-Jones 3rd

To see Rowan's portfolio turn to page 76

Joseph Burrows (16)
Barnsley

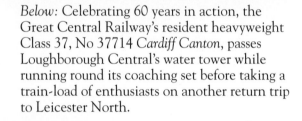

My photographs reflect a post-Covid railway, featuring both heritage and main-line steam, heritage diesels and a 'Pendolino' celebrating Pride as the world and railway return to 'normal' in different scenes and situations. The pandemic certainly inspired my photographs as I returned to travelling on the rails in May 2021, as I wanted to capture scenes of the railway recovering from the previous 14 months of disruption.

The photographs are a diverse collection from different areas of our railway network. My interpretation of the competition theme was to capture as many different scenes as possible post-lockdown, varying from returning heritage railway operations to main-line services operating day-to-day in an ever-changing world of regular or special operations.

Above: Proudly departing from Crewe, Avanti West Coast's 'Progress Train' No 390119 shows off its stunning 'Pride' livery while working a service for London Euston.

Below: Celebrating 60 years in action, the Great Central Railway's resident heavyweight Class 37, No 37714 *Cardiff Canton*, passes Loughborough Central's water tower while running round its coaching set before taking a train-load of enthusiasts on another return trip to Leicester North.

Left: LMS Ivatt Class 2MT 2-6-2T 41241 whistles over the viaduct heading towards Mytholmes Tunnel on the Keighley & Worth Valley Railway while working the 12.30 ex-Keighley service bound for Oxenhope.

Above: LMS 'Royal Scot' Class No 6115 *Scots Guardsman* reverses out of Carlisle with its support coach while on a turning move so it could face south to lead the return leg of West Coast Railway's 'The Pendle Dalesman' rail tour to Preston.

Top right: A sight now gone but never forgotten: East Midlands Railway's No 43102 *The Journey Shrinker* stands proudly at Sheffield preparing to work the 11.44 service to London St Pancras.

Right: Climbing the gradient out of Barnsley, Direct Rail Services' No 37423 leads the Branch Line Society's 'The Primary Colours' rail tour up the Penistone line towards Huddersfield, running 72 minutes late.

Jack Callaway (18)
Consett

Below: BR 'J27' No 65894 departs from Leyburn on the Wensleydale Railway.

Above: National Coal Board 'Austerity' No 49 at the Tanfield Railway.

Left: 'TPE' Class 185 unit No 185141 at Durham.

Right: LNER 'B1' No 1264 leaves Grosmont on the North Yorkshire Moors Railway.

YOUNG RAILWAY PHOTOGRAPHER OF THE YEAR

Under 19 portfolio: Ben Taylor 2nd

To see Ben's portfolio turn to page 180

Stanley Carr (17)
Gullane

Right: Farewell 'No 9'.

Below right: Out of the shelter, into the storm.

Below: Skoda attacks Shap.

Above: The 'Royal Scot'.

Right: Testing the rails.

Far right: HSTs put to rest.

Sam Carragher (16)
Newhaven

Right: Alresford station, occupied by soldiers.

Far right: A soldier looks out of the window while leaving Alresford.

Below: SR 'Q' Class No 30541 on the Bluebell Railway.

Alec Chantler (11) Golcar

'Lego train'

Max Cheek (14)
Weymouth

CrossCounty HST No 43366 speeds through Westbury.

No 35018 *British India Line* prepares to climb Upwey bank working between Weymouth and London Victoria.

Safety note: Whilst the photograph (right) was taken from a position of safety the observer on the bridge is clearly not in place of safety. (Please also refer to page 133)

Top left: No 387171 stops at Swindon while working between Bristol Parkway and London Paddington.

Top right: No 37425 *Concrete Bob* speeds through Basingstoke with a ballast engineering train.

Bottom left: A GBRf Class 66 speeds through Westbury on a light loco move to Dr Days Junction.

Above: Colas Rail Class 66s (numbers unknown) shunt around Eastleigh Yard.

Gwion Clark (18)
Conwy

The Railway Photographic Society
incorporating the
Rail Camera Club

Special award

I am a mechanical engineering student and have had a passion for railways for as long as I can remember. My interest in photography probably began with seeing my father's slides, often showing railways as they were in the past. The camera I currently use is a Nikon D3400, usually with the Nikkor AF-P 18-55mm lens. My photography is mainly about recording things as they are today, my favourite topics being railways, architecture and landscapes. Alongside the theme of 'Railways Seen' and diversity, I decided to challenge myself further by setting a theme of 'motion' for my set of six photographs; this allowed me to be creative and made me look at the railway scene from different perspectives. The theme of the old and new also runs through this diverse set of photographs, portraying the railways of the UK as they are today. The photographs show different scenes, locations, structures and traction.

Each photograph was taken handheld with a relatively slow shutter speed to gain the desired effects. Some took a little more practice than others, and also include Photoshop adjustments such as levels, highlights, contrast, sharpness and dehaze sliders adjusted to bring out details, and cropping to better frame the image. I hope you enjoy seeing them as much I did producing them!

Above: The 17.37 service from Preston departs for Blackpool North on 29 October 2019 – a slow shutter speed in low light creates an interesting effect.

Left: A colourful autumnal scene at South Gosforth showing the older and the newer as passengers make their way over the footbridge on 27 October 2021.

Right: An intentional camera movement photograph shows the modern concourse ceiling of London King's Cross from the perspective of a passenger on 8 July 2021.

Left: Busy commuters alighting from and boarding a train underneath the grand trainshed at Newcastle, as seen from the footbridge across Platform 4 on 25 October 2021.

Right: Through the gap: old and new at Carlisle on 9 October 2021.

Below: Blanche heads across Gwyndy Bank between Minffordd and Penrhyndeudraeth on the Ffestiniog Railway on 5 August 2021.

Daniel Clay (15)
London

Above: The magnificent architecture of an empty King's Cross in the late evening.

Top left: Class 43 HST No 43062 *John Armitt* at Paddington station, wearing a yellow colour scheme.

Centre left: An LNER Class 801 'Azuma' unit rests under the night lights of King's Cross station.

Bottom left: Direct Rail Services Class 57 No 57306 rests at Paddington's Platform 1 under night lights after arriving from the Reading Train Care Depot. This service reverses, then heads off to Penzance as a GWR 'Night Riviera' service hauled by another Class 57 locomotive.

Charlie Cox (16)
Taunton

Right: Awaiting departure, West Somerset Railway.

Above: 'Sprinter' at night.

Below: CrossCountry to the south.

Adam Davies (18)
Witney

I have always had a great interest in steam locomotives, and photographing them, so this competition has provided a great way to showcase this. I don't really have much of a technique, or any influences. I just show up, point a camera, and click.

All of my photos feature steam locomotives. They are a big part in my life and I will always go out for any chance to photograph or video them. This sometimes means cycling a rather long distance to achieve a good photo.

My photos are all the 'railway seen', but you have to know when and where to see it.

Right: No 7820 *Dinmore Manor* stands at Toddington on the Gloucestershire Warwickshire Railway.

Far right: No 60103 *Flying Scotsman* prepares to depart from Newbury Racecourse.

Right: No 46100 *Royal Scot* accelerates away from Oxford (IPhone SE, Stikbot tripod).

Far right: Three locomotives stand in the entrance to the locomotive shed at Didcot Railway Centre.

Louise Decelle (9) London

I moved to England from France when I was 4, and if I could describe myself in three words it would it be fun, creative and imaginative. I have always liked photography and have been interested in the different art that it creates, my favourite things to photograph being transport and nature.

I really enjoyed this project. It was part of a series of homework tasks set by my teacher, and when I saw that I could enter a photography competition I knew that would be the first task I would complete I liked the overall concept of the theme and wanted to each image to tell a story.

I chose these photographs because of the shades and the colours of each image, the way in which they complement each other, and I liked the way they show the interlinking of railway line. My favourites are 'Dark dock', because of the difference in shade and light, and 'Curves and perspective' because one of my favourite lessons at school is Maths. I like the fact that I can see shapes coming to life in this picture.

Living in London, I sometimes take for granted how accessible tubes, trains and transport are. This series reminded me of the beauty of transport and how even though to some people it is just a way to get around, I loved looking through that to the beauty in the way that the engineering comes together to pack patterns and shapes.

Above: Lancaster Gate .

Opposite page: Notting Hill Gate, curves and perspective.

Left: Notting Hill Gate.

Charlie Dent (14)
Thornton Cleveleys

Right: No 390138 at Crewe on 30 October 2021.

Below left: WMR Class 172 at Vigo Bridge on 12 August 2021.

Bottom left: No 31466 at Bridgnorth on 2 October 2021.

Below : No 5542 at Buckfastleigh on 18 August 2021.

Bottom right: No 170512 at Bromsgrove on 9 August 2021.

Opposite page: No 166212 at Dawlish on 17 August 2021.

Ryan Edge (16)
Bathgate

What excites me most about the pictures I have submitted is how well they all turned out next to similar pictures I have seen posted on Instagram, and from which I had taken inspiration. My love for the Forth Bridge also influenced two of the picture locations.

I made sure that, while including a train, all the pictures have a natural or scenic aspect to them with sunset, changing seasons and stunning landscapes. Each has a different aspect representing the 'railway seen', be it scenic, infrastructure or commuters, while also including a train.

Left: No 334028, with No 334003 on the rear, is seen working a service from Garscadden to Edinburgh past Hillend Reservoir with a threatening sky lurking above.

*Bottom far left:*Nos 47828 and 47805 pass Princes Street Gardens, Edinburgh, with 'The Statesman'.

Bottom left: No 43046, with No 43055 on the rear, works the 'Royal Highland Pullman' from St Pancras International to Inverness.

Right: No 60163 *Tornado* makes her way towards Inverkeithing with the afternoon 'Forth Circle'.

Below: A trio of Class 158s emerge from the Forth Bridge.

Below right: Unit No 385043 pulls into Livingston South as the sun sets in the background.

Peter Evans (16)
Chester

The photographs I have submitted reflect how I see the railway. While it is a form of transport, it also captures the hearts of many in the variety of traction it employs. I aim for a range of aspects when it comes to my railway photography. From a view of commuters to an enthusiasts' favourite, the pictures depict how much variety there is within the railway, from rail tour traction going back decades to today's sleek and modern express passenger trains.

With the wide range of perspectives people have of the railway, whether it is to get from 'A to B' or as a way to experience the world from a window seat, these pictures show the range of ways that people see 'the iron road'.

Right: A TransPennine Express 'Nova 1' stands in Manchester Piccadilly, on the last leg of its journey to Manchester Airport, underneath a wintry sunset on 17 January 2020.

Right: No 70000 *Britannia* surges past Winwick Junction, Warrington, with 'The Fellsman', the first steam tour out of lockdown, on 15 July 2020.

Opposite page top left: The cooling towers of Ratcliffe-upon-Soar power station dominate the skyline as No 43484 arrives at East Midlands Parkway with a southbound EMR HST service in 17 July 2020.

Opposite page bottom left: A TPE 'Nova' accelerates out of Manchester Victoria towards Miles Platting forming a service to Newcastle on 7 September 2020.

Above: No 86259 *Les Ross* awaits departure from Preston to take the 'Cumbrian Mountain Express' back to Euston on 10 October 2020.

Right: No 60163 *Tornado* powers towards Wavertree Technology Park on the return leg of 'The Ticket To Ride' rail tour from Darlington North Road to Liverpool Lime Street on 19 September 2020.

Lucinda Farrell (12)
Lytham St Annes

I love photography because I love capturing an image and being able to keep it forever, to hold on to that memory. I also love editing photos to make them different from the original image. Black and white pictures look so classic even if the original image is so modern.

My pictures show Glenfinnan Viaduct. We went there when on a summer holiday in Scotland, and I wanted to see it as it is the same bridge where 'Harry Potter' was filmed, and I'm a huge Harry Potter fan. When we got there I realised that the bridge was not only iconic but also very beautiful and very peaceful. I took loads of pictures that day because no matter when angle I used, the viaduct still looked stunning.

In this photo series I follow the 'Jacobite' on its journey across the viaduct to Glenfinnan station, where I took the picture of my sister with the impressive engine. The day started with excitement, then anticipation as we waited for the train the pass over the viaduct. It was worth the wait.

When you think of trains in Scotland, you think of the 'Jacobite'; it's the most iconic train, and has been made more popular by the 'Harry Potter' films. The steam train is so powerful and iconic, and the sounds it makes are just how you imagine a train would sound.

Callum Feeney (12) Basildon

All these pictures were taken at Tamworth on 12 August 2021.

Right: A Freightliner Class 70 passes Tamworth.

Below: CrossCountry Class 221.

Below right: DB Class 90s.

Above: An ex-London Midland Class 350 unit.

Above right: A DB Class 60.

Right: An Avanti West Coast Class 390.

Nevindie Fernando (12)
Prescot

Ever since I was little I have loved to take photos, and whenever I go somewhere I always take my phone with me to take pictures. I prefer to take pictures of the surrounding nature or the way people act – they don't have to be photogenic or picturesque.

I went to Wales with some

family friends and took some photos for my own enjoyment. I think that from a photo of normality you can infer much more than from a 'selfie'. I happen to have a passion for taking photos!

Left: The journey begins…

Above: Country railway.

Right: A railway smile.

Left: The engine I called Thomas.

Right: The iron road.

Below: Panorama.

Elliot Feuillade (15) Ferryhill

I am a keen photographer and still fairly new to the hobby, but my skills are quickly progressing. My passion for trains started at a very young age when I set up a train set in my room consisting of a few locomotives. I later sold this layout and after a few years wanted to get back into the world of trains –at the age of 14 I picked up my first camera and took it to a local level crossing to try take a few photos of commonplace trains. Now photography has taken me all over the UK chasing planes, trains and automobiles. I have been slowly but surely teaching myself how to use a camera over this time and how to bring my photos to life. Now, just one and a bit years on, I feel I have met amazing people and developed my passion for trains overall.

My selected pictures excite me in many ways, giving me a chance to express an aspect of diversity in the railway and how interesting it is once you take a deeper look into it. I got inspiration from railway magazines I saw as a child and many posts on Instagram and Facebook. I then taught myself how to operate a DSLR camera properly and went from there.

The photographs show how much diversity there is on our railways today and how there is more than meets the eye. They includes the three main types of traction – diesel, electric, and steam. They also incorporate design aspects and some of the most iconic designs of the railway and how they have progressed over the years.

Above: No 43102 sits at the National Railway Museum after a hard working life.

Bottom left: No 56006 is seen at an East Lancashire Railway Diesel Gala.

Below: A GWR IET passes the Malvern Hills.

Right: No 60103 *Flying Scotsman* is seen during a move to the NRM. (The picture was taken from an unmanned public crossing.)

Below: No 91130 makes a light engine move to Edinburgh.

Below right: No 60074 trundles along the East Coast Main Line.

Leo Fleming (10)
Canterbury

I absolutely love trains and railways because they are fascinating and there are so many individual special features that are great to take photos of. I enjoy photography because it allows me to capture one moment in time, then I can always look back at it whenever I want to. I like to find interesting and unusual views and

Far left: The footplate of *Flying Scotsman*, my favourite engine.

Left: The Mail Rail at the Postal Museum – old tiny trains and tunnels! – photographed before I had a ride through the tunnel.

Bottom far left: The view from the cab as I passed through the train wash at Selhurst Depot.

Bottom left: The escalator at the new Crossrail station at Canary Wharf.

Right: I wrote to Selhurst Train Depot to ask if I could come and have a look round. They gave me a tour and it was one of the best days of my life!

Above: No 60103 *Flying Scotsman* seen from the front. The best steam locomotive!

some of the most unusual opportunities I have had to take photos of the railway world have been when I have asked to visit behind the scenes, like when I wrote a letter to Selhurst Depot and had a tour of the entire depot.

My selected pictures reflect the variety on the railway and show so many different aspects. I get excited by exploring the history of railways in the UK, such as the Mail Rail train, as well as being able to see brand-new developments like the Crossrail station at Canary Wharf. My photography is also inspired by my all-time favourite engines like *Flying Scotsman*, and being able to go on the footplate was amazing!

This series of photographs is all about the different ways the railway can be seen, past, present and future, especially behind the scenes – all these different aspects are just as important.

Courtenay Forder (18)
Ashford

My interest in photography started at a young age. I used to have a little digital camera that I used when out and about. When I became older I got a little more creative with my photos and my Dad picked up on the fact that I was getting more interested, but it wasn't until I started using my phone more often that I realised there maybe something to this. I started working alongside a railway YouTuber and I ended up with a Canon DSLR, and the interest carried on.

I love the history that comes with all locomotives. My inspiration came from my family – my Dad loved taking me to heritage railways while I was growing up, and when I was given my camera I just took to it like a duck to water!

I have tried to provide a mixture of engines working hard as well as the overall landscape. I get around to a lot of different heritage railways, so have tried to include a mixture of different locomotives. The general public don't always see what goes on behind the scenes on those railways, or appreciate what photos can be obtained if you know where to stand or if the lighting hits in just the right place. These pictures were taken with a Samsung phone.

Above: 'Q' Class No 30541 stands in front of 'Standard 5' *Camelot*, posing as *Linette*, on the Bluebell Railway at the end of the Giants of Steam weekend, 13 October 2019.

Left: 'Terrier' tank No 32678 returns to Rolvenden on 23 February 2019.

Right: 'USA' 'S100' tank No 30070, currently posing as *Frank S. Ross* on the Kent & East Sussex Railway, is seen on New Year's Day.

Matthew Fraser (17) Uxbridge

My photography is mainly inspired by Colin Gifford, and the pictorialist movement of the 1800s – I particularly enjoy using antique and vintage photographic equipment to photograph railway-related subjects.

What excites me about this selection of pictures is the range of trains, from main-line steam in odd locations to London Underground's battery locomotives, a rare sight in daylight. I was particularly inspired by Colin Gifford's approach, and how all of his work was shot using analogue techniques, almost creating a pictorialist set of images. I wanted to convey a wide range of subjects, from narrow-gauge steam engine built for the joy of it to purely utilitarian locomotives such as a Rail Operations Group Class 37.

Among these photos are images of trains around London, with a focus on modern main-line steam and the trains operated by Transport for London. Within the competition's theme I wanted to convey the rapidly changing face of Britain's railways, and the effects of privatisation. I also wanted to include strong contrasts, for example a highly polished LNER locomotive running beneath a rusting footbridge. Another example is a near-60-year-old diesel locomotive delivering new trains for the Elizabeth Line in London. I felt it was especially important to include steam engines in this series, to show that despite their age they can still power on and fit within a modern network.

Above: London Underground battery locomotive No L49 passes through West Ham station.

Below: Central Line train interior.

Top: ROG Class 37 No 37601 leads new Crossrail unit No 345017 at Stratford.

Above: LNER Thompson Class 'B1' No 61306 *Mayflower* on the Greenford Triangle.

Jago Frost (14)
Hereford

Growing up along the East Lancashire Railway, I have always had a firm interest in railways, and am fascinated by their operation and the engineering details behind them. In particular, I like Regional and Inter-City rail, and enjoy deliberating on how to improve services in both fields. All the photos submitted were taken on a Canon EOS 350D, and I generally do not edit my photos, as is the case with all those here.

For as long as I can remember I have found trains incredibly exciting. I never edit my pictures and hope that these photographs provide a capsule of the moments in which they were taken. It excites me to record unremarkable day-to-day events, with the knowledge that the obscure services I have ridden in the past will not be lost to history.

The selection contains photos taken from different viewpoints, and aims to represent the diversity of the network. That said, all the photographs feature very few people, partly by necessity given the pandemic, but mainly to represent a quiet and often neglected industry, keeping the country running in the background. In particular they depict one of the quietest years the railway has had over its history, and I have tried to convey the unfamiliar desolation over much of the network, even after restrictions had been eased, capturing the settings as they really were.

Above: Running light engine, a DB Class 66 passes through Newport as a pair of GWR IETs departs for Cardiff.

Below left: Bury Bolton Street station on the East Lancashire Railway, August 2020.

Below right: Two LNER Class 801s pass between Darlington and York.

Left: A London North Western Railway Class 350 unit leaves Crewe bound for London on 26 July 2020.

Right: A rural scene at Stoke Edith, Herefordshire, lit by a late-afternoon sun in October 2021.

Below: Worcester Shrub Hill station in August 2021. Taken at about a quarter to eight, it was already dark, but a relatively long exposure makes it appear much brighter.

Alfie Gascoigne (15) Gateshead

Since a very young age I have been passionate about and extremely interested in transport, trains and how they operate – and of course I take photos of transport as a result. I have done this since I was young, when I'd be out on the Metro with my family and my KidiZoom camera, which was great!

I have always loved to take photos of railways, including some sort of alternative close-up photos of the mechanisms of trains and locomotives. My selection is variety of photos from a trip to Carlisle and the close-ups of the steam loco that I saw there. There's also a view from the side of a train carriage on the Tanfield Railway, where I volunteer in all of my spare time.

I have a firm belief that the railways should be seen from multiple perspectives, and not just 'from the platform', hence my series of photos show a variety of different locations and angles.

Left: An 'Azuma' on a dark night.

Far left bottom: Forty years of IC125s.

Right: The Tanfield Railway.

Far right: *British India Line* – up close.

Below left: The Tanfield Railway on a summer day.

Below: The firebox.

Shane Gopal (17)
Peterborough

Far right: No 390104 passes Rugeley in heavy rain.

Right: Nos 86637 and 86622 run through Rugeley.

Below: No 37254 passes through Lincoln.

Left: No 90001 passes Yaxley Lode, Peterborough.

Right: 88006 passing Rugeley.

Below: No 91102 passes New Zealand Bridge.

Joseph Graham (18)
Stockport

I'm an autistic 18-year-old photographer, and have always been interested in trains. I love everything about them, from how they work to how they look. As I became older I got into trainspotting with my friends and taking photographs and videos of various types of trains for my YouTube channel and Instagram page. I've been passionate about photography for some years now and I'm glad that both of my interests fit together so well. I use varied types of devices to take photos, often using my IPad or phone, but also my camera from time to time. My techniques vary depending on the location and subject; if it's a locomotive that is named I always like to try and get a decent photo of the nameplate. I also like to try different angles and points of view to make the photo look right in my eyes, but also to make it appealing to others when they look at my work.

What excites me about me about my series is that it captures a few parts of railway life today from different types of trains and infrastructure such as stations and it represents what it's like in the eyes of railway enthusiasts. My inspiration comes from other spotters looking at people's photos in magazines or online gives me the drive to capture a certain locomotive that may have been in that photo.

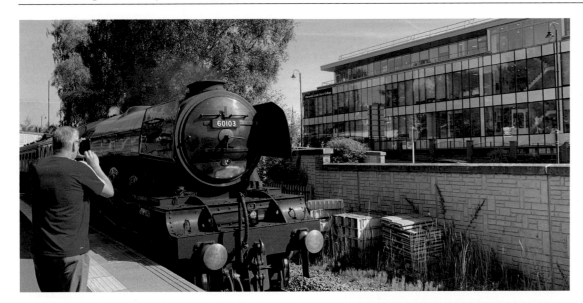

My selection of pictures contains different aspects of railway life at different times of the year, as well as showing different parts of the railway scene: steam and diesel charters, modern freight locos keeping the everyday network running, and a station before a beautiful backdrop.

Top left: 46100 *Royal Scot* on 15 February 2021.

Far left: Platform 2 at Romiley station on 2 April 2021.

Left: The Red Beast of England, Scotland and Wales, on 9 August 2021.

Above: *Flying Scotsman* at speed, 23 August 2021.

Top right: 'A1' No 60163 *Tornado* at Stockport on 23 March 2019.

Right: The Tractor and The Bodysnatcher on tour with the *Retro Cumbrian Coaster II* at Stockport, 28 August 2021.

Edison Green (10)
Whitley Bay

Ihave been fascinated by trains ever since receiving a wooden Brio set as a toddler. Now, as a 10-year-old, my interest is stronger than ever. I am particularly passionate about the environmental benefits trains can bring over other forms of transport, especially through electrification.

This interest is combined with photography and travelling to new places, making railway photography the perfect hobby. I love to visit beautiful locations in the UK and abroad, stopping at scenic stations and viewpoints wherever I am.

I like the photographs I have submitted because they show a contrast between old and new on the railway in a rural part of the country, in this case steam and diesel trains near Weybourne on the North Norfolk Railway. My inspiration came from photos in magazines like *Steam World* about the end of steam, and from *The Railway Magazine*'s article about the competition.

Far left: Diesel trains at the shed at Weybourne.

Far left bottom: A diesel multiple unit stabled at Weybourne.

Left: A Class 31 arriving at Weybourne.

Bottom left: The green-liveried Class 31 leaves Weybourne. Note in the background some offshore wind turbines.

Below: The Class 31 and a steam-hauled train at Weybourne.

Right: A Class 37 and a steam train at Weybourne in driving rain.

Tom Halliwell (13) Dewsbury

Right: Teamwork.

Far right:
Underground but
overground.

Below left: The city
of Leeds.

Below right: Cloudy
Yorkshire.

Welcome to Cornwall.

Daniel Hanham (15)
York

Left: No 68031 *Felix*, accompanied by Mk5a set TP10, accelerates out of York on a journey from Scarborough to Manchester Victoria, which was only running a couple of times per day in April 2021 due to the Covid-19 reduced timetable.

Right: No 90001 *Royal Scot*, in its Intercity Swallow livery, is seen at Platform 1 at York towards the end of September 2020, waiting for Jeremy Hosking's private tour to arrive from Scotland.

Far left bottom: As they pass under the iconic signal box at Hexham, Nos 800201 and 801105 work along the Tyne Valley route towards Carlisle in October 2021 with a service that will eventually reach Aberdeen multiple hours later because of the scheduled diversions away from the East Coast Main Line.

Bottom left: Old meets new as unit No 158902 coasts into Platform 1 at Whitby while Class 'S15' No 825 sits in Platform 2 in front of the new housing development in the seaside town, awaiting the return of its passengers before it sets off back to Pickering on the 'Optimist' trip on Friday 30 October 2020.

Above: Unit No 158848 crosses Knaresborough Viaduct as it comes to the end of its journey along the Harrogate Line from Leeds, seen from in front of Knaresborough Castle in April 2021.

Left: No D4 (44004) *Great Gable* exits Orton Mere on a Peterborough to Wansford journey on Day 2 of the 'Three Peaks Challenge Diesel Gala' in early October 2021.

Rowan Harris-Jones (17)
Berwick Upon Tweed

I have always had a passion for trains and railways, especially capturing them through a lens. This started at the age of three when we lived close to the Settle & Carlisle railway, and my Nana would often take me to see trains. At the age of 13 I was given my first DSLR camera, and most of my railway images were focussed around the Berwick and Borders area, having moved to Northumberland. It was around this time that I also started helping as a volunteer at the Aln Valley Railway. At the age of 16 I left school having studied Photography at GCSE and have been studying Rail Engineering at Newcastle College since then.

I like to specialise in pictures of trains within the landscape, and over the last few years have travelled across the country to capture images, a number of which have been published. My photography trips are now highly planned, looking at weather conditions, sun angles and locations as well as unusual train movements to make my images unique and interesting; this also enables me to understand the story behind the image and place it in context. I am inspired by the stunning landscapes that the trains are travelling through, the colours, the setting, and ultimately what train is being captured.

I love getting out and about, meeting really inspiring photographers who have taught me new skills and allowed me to develop my photography techniques. I get really excited when I get home and download the photographs onto the big screen – then I can really see what I have managed to capture through the viewfinder.

Above: With the rail scene ever changing, I like to try and photograph ageing rolling stock, soon to be sitting in sidings with an uncertain future. Colas Rail Class 37s Nos 37057 and 37612 pass the gallery at Little Fenton on 23 August while working 1Q62, the West Yorkshire Test Train.

Below: Colas Rail Class 56 No 56096 crosses the Royal Border Bridge in the last light of the longest day of the year working 6S95, the 13.47 Sinfin to Grangemouth empty aviation tanks.

Right: I like illustrating ever-changing landscapes such as this scene, now consigned to the history books. DB Cargo No 60001 passes the soon to be demolished Lackenby steelworks while working 6D11, the 13.19 Lackenby to Scunthorpe steel empties, on 15 April.

Above: Rail Operations Group Class 37s Nos 37510, 37800 and 57312 are seen snaking their way around the Cumbrian coast passing through Nethertown working the 'Retro Cumbrian Coaster II', the 1Z30 Workington to Chesterfield train, on 28 August.

Below: Taken at one of my favourite locations, and featuring one of my favourite locomotives, LSL Nos 47805 and 47853 are seen passing Spittal working 1Z37, the 09.20 Inverness to Ely, returning from a weekend in the Highlands on 27 September 27.

Below: I also like capturing the modern railway scene in different seasons. Here ROG No 47812 heads 5E23, Slateford to Doncaster Wabtec, consisting of a rake of newly refurbished ScotRail Mk 3s, through a snowy wintery scene on 10 February.

Joseph Hart (14)
Newton Abbot

'Preserved Pacer'.

Little engines can do big things.

What interests me in railway photography is when I capture the perfect photo in the perfect location, whether it's a steam train storming up a bank or a diesel thrashing through the countryside. On the other hand, a diesel train also looks the part when stationary while waiting for the green light. I take my inspiration from finding new locations that offer good composition and lighting. The technique I like to use is to get the whole train in view and take in enough scenery, which I feel is really important to make a great photograph. On every visit I make to any railway, whether it is a heritage railway or main line, there is always something different or unusual happening – no two days are the same and this is what motivates my photography.

These photographs were taken around Devon. They have different compositions with locomotives and locations ranging from Scottish Standards to preserved 'Pacers' from Paignton to Plymouth.

Right: Devonshire delight.

Clagtastic! Scottie in Devon *Above*:

Rhubarb and custard.

The return of the 'Blue Pullman'.

Edward Harvey (16) Sheffield

Following the Covid lockdowns, I was keen to get back out photographing railways. One place I have frequented has been the Great Central Railway. I aimed to capture the feel of a 'bygone age' with my photographs. I was also keen to photograph the current railway scene, such as people making their way to their train. I wanted to try and capture people in my shots as this has been something absent for the last 18 months.

The photographs range from the reopening of heritage railways to the return of leisure travel on the National Network. I tried to include people in my shots and capture the railway as a passenger would view it, from their train at the platform, doors open, to a crowded platform for a long-distance journey and the romance of heritage steam.

Top left: Looking up the Great Central, from bridge 336 towards Quorn & Woodhouse.

Far left: A steam-hauled service departs from Quorn & Woodhouse.

Left: Ivatt 2MT No 46521 on shed at Loughborough.

Above: A Northern Class 195 unit standing at Dore & Totley waiting to depart for Sheffield.

Above right: A CrossCountry HST pulls into a rather busy Sheffield station on its long journey to the West Country.

Right: Enthusiasts return to their train at Leicester North, having photographed the locomotive run-round.

Samuel Haworth (10)
Bexleyheath

When I turned 10 I asked for my own DSLR camera after learning how to use my Daddy's camera. I used my love of railways and history to develop my knowledge of techniques, lenses and shutter speeds to frame the beauty in front of me. My wish was to have a camera that could capture my love of trains in detail so I could remember fun-filled family days and share my love of trains with my like-minded grandpas. I have had a lifelong love of trains and history and wish to become a railway historian in the future, starting by recording in photography my favourite engines.

I have loved heritage railways all my life since seeing my first steam train when I was just one! My love of heritage railways and history led me to look at railways through history. I loved the contrast been the Victorian era trains and the more modern-day diesels, and the shared enjoyment that trains, both standard and narrow gauge, bring to all ages and communities. While modern trains speed past and often their beauty is lost, the heritage railways allow us to take time, relax and reflect on how humans have gone from horses to powerful dragon-like engines in less than two centuries. My selection of photographs thus focuses on the contrast between old and new, and different sizes.

A contrast between the beauty of *Flying Scotsman* and the practicality of the more modern but now redundant 'Pacer' trains.

Below left and below: The splendour of a South African Garratt engine in typical contrasting grey Welsh weather.

workhorses of the railway in the shunting yard working together to
n the engine shed.

s 47 diesel *County of Essex* in full throttle flying past *Flying Scotsman*!

How a design in miniature can be perfect and so strong!

Dylan Heggie (18) Edinburgh

I have autism and transport has always been one of my main interests and hobbies. When I was younger I really enjoyed going on train and bus trips and visiting transport museums. For my 16th birthday I got a camera, and this has helped me to develop my interest in transport photography; taking photos of trains and buses helps me to focus on the subject and this helps me to reduce and control my anxiety that forms part of my autism.

Right: No 91107 *Skyfall* is seen in the 'mirror' windows opposite Platform 5 at Edinburgh Waverley on 12 October 2019.

Below: MPV DR98911 turning on to the Edinburgh South Suburban line at Slateford, working a train from Fort William. It was photographed from Slateford station on 10 May 2019.

Below right: DRS No 66426 has just arrived at Bo'ness on 28 December 2019, with InterCity-liveried No 47643 and BR Blue No 26038 on the back, during the Bo'ness & Kinniel Railway Diesel Gala.

Above: No 91102 *City of York* stands at Platform 5 at Edinburgh Waverley on 19 December 2019.

Left: CrossCountry unit No 221128 arrives at a busy Edinburgh Waverley station on 19 October 2019.

Right: Mk3 TS 42234, repainted in 1970s BR blue for the LNER HST farewell rail tour 'Let's Go Round Again', was photographed at Edinburgh on 19 December 2019.

Liam Hetherington (13)
London

My favourite trains and locomotives are 'Pacers', Class 37s, HSTs and Class 91s. I like taking pictures of trains and sunsets.

This selection of photographs excites me because it includes my favourite trains, and is also a reflection of my hard work; it is the first time I have tried abstract photography and have experimented with some new techniques. I have also managed to photograph some rare trains. Finally it has inspired to go to see interesting locations and trains.

The pictures show a range of subjects in terms of age, setting and photographic technique, including picturesque and urban settings.

I interpreted the theme by photographing a variety of locomotives and trains of various ages – the very old Class 37, the 'medium old' Class 66 and the very new 'Meridian'.

Reflections on a 'Meridian'.

'Tractor' in the woods.

Graffiti 'Shed'.

YOUNG RAILWAY PHOTOGRAPHER OF THE YEAR

Under 19 portfolio: 1st Sean Mattocks

To see Sean's complete portfolio turn to page 124

John Vincent Heywood (14)
Aberdeen

I have been photographing steam trains since I was three, when we were on holiday in Devon. I liked to stand on the footbridge at Buckfastleigh station – my family called it 'John's bridge'. My first camera was a toy camera from my sister. I got my first proper camera when I was five, a Panasonic bridge camera. It had a massive built-in zoom lens, which I really liked, but it was very hard to get a moving train in the right place because there was a small delay after you pressed the shutter release.

When I was eight in 2015 my Dad got a new camera, and he gave me his old one. It was a Nikon D-3100 with an 18-55mm zoom lens. Now I have a similar Nikon D-3300, and I like to borrow my Dad's 70-200mm zoom lens. My favourite engine is *Duchess of Sutherland*.

For me railway photographs are about the steam train subject, the surroundings, the framing and especially the light, and I chose these pictures because they all have that combination. I would have liked to include a long-lens shot, but I don't have any from 2019-21 with really nice lighting. I learned about glint lighting when I was very young, and I like to try to get a glint whenever I can.

My selection shows steam trains in different parts of northern Scotland. My favourite line is the Kyle line, but I don't have any sunny pictures there. I chose these pictures because they were taken in nice light and include everything I aim for in a good photo. The series also shows three lines that are very different from each other.

Right and opposite upper left and lower left: Three pictures were taken during a family weekend holiday. On the Saturday we went to the West Highland line and the sun came out for the afternoon 'Jacobite' train to Mallaig. It was September 2020 so the sun was quite low, and I really wanted to capture the glint on the train. My favourite photo is the 'portrait'-format one: I really like the contrast between the colours of the sky and the sea, both being different shades of blue. I also like how the rocky mountains add depth to the photo. I was really pleased to capture the glint on the engine and carriages as well.

Right: Arbroath 'smokie'! This was a lucky chance at Arbroath in July 2021. (An 'Arbroath smokie' is a smoked haddock.)

Below: On the Sunday we went to the Strathspey Railway, and this is the first train in the woods at Aviemore. I went for a landscape approach to create a frame of greenery.

Chay Hinton (16) Scarborough

I was born in Birmingham but relocated to Scarborough at the age of seven. I have had a love of trains for my whole life – I love everything to do with them, from modelling to visiting heritage lines. From an early age I have collected model trains and have recently joined a model railway club. I have also visited the majority of heritage lines in the UK, which over the years has fuelled my love of trains. During a recent visit to the National Railway Museum (one of many), I discovered a love of photographing trains. Since then I have been borrowing my grandfather's camera in order to photograph trains as often as possible. I regularly spend many days visiting various stations and locations in order to photograph trains, and I also film footage for my YouTube channel (TPE Railfan). Although I am still fairly new to photography I very much look forward to spending many years to come developing my photography skills.

I love nothing more than to spend the day photographing trains. You never know what you are going to see – every day is different. When I photographed the Class 803 I was so excited I couldn't stand still! In these photographs you will see a mixture of old and new locomotives and trains, providing a good rounded representation of the types of trains and things to see on the railways both today and in days gone by.

Above: Old and new: 'The Scarborough Spa Express' being pulled by LMS 'Jubilee' No 45562 *Alberta/Galatea* being passed by a TPE 'Nova 3' on 30 July2020.

Below left: Brand-new 'Lumo' No 803003 doing a test run under the headcode on 16 October 2021.

Below: LNER 'Azuma' No 801219 passes Colton Junction on 24 June 2020.

Above: West Coast Railways No 47772 pulls a broken-down *Flying Scotsman* through Colton Junction on 19 June 2021.

Above right: BR Green No D1755 double-heads with BR Blue No 20189 on a special from Scarborough to Tyseley on 25 August 2021.

Right: SR 'Merchant Navy' No 35018 *British India Line*, on the 'The Lunes River Trust' special, being refuelled at Scarborough's turntable while 'Nova 3' No 68033 passes on 26 September 2021.

Nathan Hirst (13)
Houghton Le Spring

East, but also around the country when I have the chance. My selection of photographs excites me because it shows a mix of future, current and heritage trains that have been/ are being used on the network we see today. They relate to the theme of 'the railway seen' as they show trains that can be seen on the British railway network, mainly in the north of the country.

Top right: TPE grey.

Right: All together now.
Top left: 47 meets 68

Left: LNER meets Northern.

Above: 390 meets 66.

Below: CrossCountry meets ex-ScotRail.

Jacob Hooley (11) Hertford

I have had an interest in trains and transport since I was very young. My first memory of getting on a train was catching a Virgin 'Pendolino' from London Euston to Stafford to see my grandparents. When my family moved from London to Hertfordshire, I was able to see a variety of other trains such as the Greater Anglia Class 317s, and the Great Northern Class 365 'Smiley trains', as I used to call them. My interest led me to start train photography and a YouTube channel showing my films of trains (YouTube-Vehicles With Jacob). I'm so pleased that I have this hobby and I'll continue for as long as I can.

Right: A GWR Class 158 unit in the rain at Plymouth forming a service to Liskeard.

Below: A Class 317 at Broxbourne with a service to London Liverpool Street.

Top left: A Class 222 passing Harlington at speed.

Top right: An EMR Class 156 leaves Uttoxeter on a sunny day forming a service to Derby.

Right: Class 387 and Class 801 pass at Hadley Wood.

Below: Multiple trains at York (Classes 800, 221 and C180).

Matthew Howe (16)
St Ives (Cambs)

I have had a keen interest in railways since I was nine. It all started with holidays to Norfolk, travelling to Sheringham on the North Norfolk Railway and seeing such impressive machines such as 9F No 92203 *Black Prince*. Fast forward to 2018 and that's when I started trainspotting fully, using my phone to take videos and photos, seeing the Greater Anglia Class 90s as well as the final days of Virgin Trains East Coast, then the farewell to the HSTs in 2019.

I got my Canon EOS 450D in September 2020 and, with lockdown restrictions easing, I began to travel more and see and photograph other parts of the UK rail network. Although I saw the final withdrawal of HSTs from key inter-city routes in May 2021, they were not of course the only thing I made sure I saw. Class 91s were and are still my main priority, as they are by far my favourite locomotives! I don't mind seeing the more usual things, though, and love to see rarer workings!

The photographs I have selected excite me because they combine photography with good timing, some more out of the ordinary and some more original but showcasing 'celebrity' locomotives or less common movements such as test trains. They show the current diversity and changing scene of Britain's railways, with newer stock displacing older stock to storage or secondary routes, as well as others receiving 'retro' liveries they once wore. I have also tried to show a wide variety of liveries and locomotives/units not just in one area, but in many areas of the UK.

Top right: Just like old times: making their final move, former EMR HSTs Nos 43317 and 43307 cross paths with No 170105 at March, just as they would have done two years earlier with LNER during the ECML diversions.

Right: With a brief patch of sun at the perfect time and gloomy skies in the distance, two LNER 'Azumas' cross paths at Huntingdon as they both head towards their destinations.

Left: Trains, planes, but no automobiles!

Right: Sunset celebrity: LNER's Intercity 'Swallow' No 91119 *Bounds Green Intercity Depot 1977-2017* looks stunning as she powers north through Biggleswade.

Below left: The beginning of a new era. Having been withdrawn from passenger service in May, former EMR HST power cars see further work by powering test trains like this one, seen passing New Zealand Bridge with No 43274 leading and No 43272 at the rear.

Below right: Silent: once the backbone of Britain's high-speed passenger services, several former EMR HST power cars sit dormant at Ely Papworth Sidings.

Elle-May Ingham (9) Keighley

These are all photographs I have taken on holiday in Wales or near my house in Yorkshire. It's been exciting going out to take photographs of railways after all the problems with lockdown and Covid. My family are photographers, and I like going out with them to take my own pictures.

Almost all of the photographs were taken on the Keighley & Worth Valley (my local railway – I love to watch the trains come past the house, and to be able to walk up to Damems station to see them again), or the Ffestiniog and Welsh Highland Railways (near where we go on holiday most years). There is a photo taken on the main line in Wales of a special train passing a place we had a picnic, where my foster Dad used to camp when he was my age.

Because the railways I have photographed are working again after the lockdowns, it has been great to go and ride the trains and take pictures of them at the stations. The selected shots all show lines and locations that mean something to me personally; I love walking near Ribblehead, Llangollen is the local

line for some family friends who've started volunteering there, Tan-y-Bwlch is a station I've been visiting on holidays to Wales since I was four; and the Middleton is another line I've been going to from an early age.

I don't want to have just one technique or style, as I'm learning photography as I go. I see it all as an experiment, a constant learning process. I enjoy the trips out, and the chance to take photographs, even if they are just shot on my phone. They are partly just to record the day, a memory of the trip, but also an experiment, as I learn more about photography and composition.

Opposite bottom left: No 41241 in the snow at Damems, Keighley & Worth Valley Railway, winter 2020.

Left: No 41241 at Haworth Station, K&WVR, spring 2021.

Right: 'Big Jim' at Damems, K&WVR.

Below right: Below right: Yellow No 97304 (ex-No 37217) leads an unidentified classmate on the Cambrian Coast line, summer 2021.

Below: Welsh Pony at Tan-y-Bwlch, on the Ffestiniog Railway, summer 2021.

Jasmine Ingham (13)
Keighley

My pictures were mainly taken on preserved railways (except for the shot of Ribblehead Viaduct), taken on days out with my family; visits to such lines are something we regularly do as a family activity.

The photographs were taken on lines during the Covid pandemic, which influenced my taking them; visits to railways have been a feature of my life since I was very young, and though often the railways visited have been operating under restrictions, it has still felt like a little bit of normality, being able to ride trains or walk around stations. In the case of the Llangollen pictures, it's even more important to me, as this is a railway on which a close family friend volunteers, and a line that has barely survived the pandemic, but is working hard to come back to life. Visiting these lines, riding the trains, photographing them, just seems like an important thing to do right now.

Above: Llangollen station, summer 2021.

Far left: DMUs cross at the Llangollen Railway, summer 2021.

Left: A saddle tank on a freight train in the woods, Middleton Railway, autumn 2021.

Right: Northern Class 158s on Ribblehead Viaduct, summer 2020.

Above: Keighley & Worth Valley Railway: a 4F runs round at Keighley, autumn 2020.

Right: On the Ffestiniog Railway *Lyd* takes water at Tan-y-Bwlch, autumn 2021.

Max Johnston (14)
Alton

Right: 'Choppers' at Alton.

Below left: Standard Class 4 No 76017 at Alresford.

Below right: 46 xx Class 46XX 0-6-0 pannier tank at Alresford

The Judges' 'Picks' (1)

Train and plane
By Matthew Howe (16)

Rail and air travel is an issue hotly debated in today's climate-conscious society, where trains are the obvious winner for those looking to reduce their carbon footprint, if not their budget. This striking image, caught at just the right moment, underscores that debate by bringing the aircraft and the train into an uneasy relationship with each other. The photographer has used a powerful perspective to enhance the drama while the relatively grey skies allow the colours of the vehicles to pop. (See page 96)

Selhurst Depot
By Leo Fleming (10)

The surroundings of an operational main-line train depot in the British Isles are normally out of the gaze of members of the public. Judges were touched by the story behind this photograph. It is easy for enquiring minds to gaze into a depot from a passing train and ponder what might be taking place. However, for someone at such a young age to make the effort to contact a train operating company about the possibility of going behind the scenes at a depot shows remarkable initiative. It is perhaps a textbook example of the idea that if you don't ask, you don't get.

The image was no formal posed shot, perhaps providing an artificial view of the goings on – rather it was a snapshot of the daily life at the depot. It is the sort of that which might appear in a history book in years to come, providing an invaluable perspective on the past.

With a depot being a vital element of the railway, it also satisfied the infrastructure element of the theme.

The photographer may well go on to enjoy a career in the rail industry and or inspire others to do so. In that respect, it could also be said that this image shows the train operator in a positive light. (See page 58)

Ryan Kitchen (17) Featherstone

I am currently studying A-Level Photography. I first gained an interest in the railways from my Grandad who used to work as a signaller for British Rail. I also got a lot of books about the history of the railways from my Grandad. I enjoys going out with my Nikon D3300 to photograph many different steam locomotives, such as *Flying Scotsman*, *Tornado* and *Duchess of Sutherland*, as well as capturing a variety of different types of regular main-line trains such as Classes 800/801, 195 and 180. I also enjoy photographing architecture, which is currently a theme I am using within my A-Level portfolio.

Right: 'West Country' speed.

Below right: The old and the very old.

Below: The King of Steam.

I also enjoy visiting the National Railway Museum to see the different types of preserved locomotives and exhibits on display, such as *Mallard*, the 0 Series Shinkansen and *Evening Star*. I also enjoy travelling, and have visited places such as Iceland and the island of Sicily; in Iceland he got the opportunity to witness and photograph the Aurora Borealis.

What excites me about the photographs I have submitted is how technology has changed; they show a range of different locomotives, steam, diesel and electric, as well as showing the different ways in which our railways have developed through different types of rolling stock, carriages and means of power compared to 100 years ago. They reflect how our trains have evolved, with electrified lines and modern railway stations, and how they could evolve in the near future.

Right: Express LNER.

Below: Brunswick 'Streak'.

Below right: 'Azuma love'.

Rohan Konar-Thakkar (11) London

I love trains, specifically metro and light rail systems. My favourite station is Paddington, and favourite train the British Rail Class 803. My camera is my mobile phone.

What excites me about these photos (taking and editing them) is the fact that they were all taken in less than a month, all on the London Underground, and mostly following the same route, yet so varied in location and feeling. They show various London Underground stations during the peak and off-peak hours, as well as original Underground stations now served by more modern trains.

Right:
One point perspective view of a TFL Rail train.

Above right: Earl's Court London Underground station.

Left and below: The side of S7 stock, Hammersmith & City Line.

Trains arriving at St John's Wood and and departing from Broad Street London Underground stations.

James Lamb (17) Evesham

Above left: A Rail Operations Group '47'.

Above: No 9466 at Cheltenham Race Course station.

Left: *Trangkil No 4* at Statfold Barn Railway.

Right: No 2 *Roger* on the Garden Railway at Statfold Barn Railway.

Far right top: Hunslet quarry engines *Alice* and *Winifred* at the Bala Lake Railway.

Far right bottom: *Mariloo* at Exbury Gardens.

Danny Leggett (13)
Woodbridge

I've had an interest in trains for as long as I can remember, and when I'm old enough I want to be a train driver. I live in Suffolk and I've recently become a volunteer at the Mid-Suffolk Light Railway. Not long ago I had the opportunity to drive a 7¼-inch-gauge locomotive down a very short section of track.

In September 2021 I went to Bressingham's 60th anniversary gala where there were lots of trains running, including one that used to run there named *Bronllwyd*, which was Alan Bloom's favourite engine, now based at the Statfold Barn Railway. In October 2021 I went to the Mid-Norfolk Railway where the famous *Flying Scotsman* was visiting. It's an amazing locomotive and has a distinctive whistle.

I also enjoy trainspotting at my local station, Ipswich, where lately I saw several rare movements. My favourite class of locomotive is the Class 37 and my favourite steam engine is probably *Flying Scotsman*, though I do quite like Quarry Hunslets. The pictures were taken on A Canon 1200D except those at Bressingham and Dereham, where I used a Samsung Galaxy a40.

Above: A Class 755 approaches Ipswich.

Below left: A Class 88 runs light engine through Ipswich.

Below: Two Class 37s top-and-tailing on a Railhead Treatment Train pass through Ipswich.

Above: The 2-foot-gauge steam engines operational at Bressingham's 60th anniversary are seen lined up at the end of the day.

Above: One of Freightliner's Class 66s runs light engine into Ipswich Yard.

Below: The world's most famous steam locomotive, No 60103 *Flying Scotsman* is seen preparing to depart from Dereham during its visit to the Mid-Norfolk Railway.

Sofia Looker (15)
Beverley

I like to take pictures of trains due to my interest in travelling on them. I take photos to document that I have travelled on a certain train or because that particular train interests me. I have travelled on trains extensively, right from when I was a very young age. My Dad brought me into the hobby and I continued to be brought up on trains. This hobby has allowed me visit many cities around the UK and abroad, including Europe and the full length of the Trans-Siberian Railway from Vladivostok to Moscow. I always thoroughly enjoy my adventures by train, and the photographs are a permanent reminder of these times.

Opposite top: No 37423 at Wymondham Abbey on 7 April 2019.

Opposite far left: Power unit removal from No 50030 at Rowsley on 29 September 2020.

Left: Reflection of No 50008 at Dereham on 7 April 2019.

Above: No 68023 approaches York on 17 February 2019.

Above right: An LNER DVT and 'Voyager' near Durham on 10 April 2019.

Right: No 91119 at Colton Junction on 25 June 2020.

Adam Lowings (13) Mansfield

Photography has been an interest of mine since being lucky enough to use my Dad's Nikon D70 at the age of four – I remember it being too heavy for me to hold properly. As I learn more about photography I have experimented more with my cameras. My latest is a Nikon D7200, which I have been using for three years. This is great for low-light stationary shots and fast daytime views. My camera rarely leaves my side and at any opportunity I'm out looking for my next capture. I love photography as I feel it is the only way to capture, freeze and record any moment in time – a passing freight train, a steam special, a local commuter service, or the latest Hitachi trains. The feeling of freedom that photography gives me is fantastic – I can create as many picture memories as I like at any moment in time.

My hobby is influenced by my family's love of travel and my Dad's interest in transport. We don't remember steam on the main line, nor like the newest of trains, but progress happens and time moves on. Capturing that moment allows it to remain in our minds for ever.

The railway is seen by me as a varied gallery of design, style, colour and companies. Each area has its own operators, its own classes. The railway scene has to be seen to be appreciated, and I capture as much of that scene as I can while working hard towards my GCSEs.

A picture is a piece of art to me and something I have created. It's special and means something to me – I've seen it and through my photos I won't forget it. It's just a shame I can't travel back in time to see steam on the main line !

Above right: Reflections at 'The Cross'.

Right: No 43183 growing old gracefully – the Scottish renaissance.

Above: No 70013 *Oliver Cromwell:* timeless serenity in motion.

Above right: No 43300 marking 100 years of Craigentinny.

Right: No 82205, a Scotsman in South Muskham.

Below: No 43295 powering towards retirement.

Jack Lye (15)
Crook

Right: Standing at Carlisle, a TPE 'Nova 2' and Class 37 No 37610.

Below: 'Voyager' at Newcastle.

Below right: A Class 66 sitting at Carlisle waiting for a green signal.

Opposite top left: Class 390 No 390043 awaits departure from Carlisle.

Opposite top right: Double 'Pacers' sitting at Darlington.

Opposite bottom: A Northern Class 153 unit at Appleby.

Ben Mackay (16) Gore Bridge

Above: No 37425 is stabled in the middle road at Ipswich awaiting departure with 3S10, Stowmarket to Stowmarket, on the night of 23 October 2020.

Right: No 37425 is seen erupting out of Southend Victoria working 3S60, Stowmarket to Stowmarket, on 22 October 2020.

Left: No 56094 triple-heads with Nos 56096 and 56105 passing Blindwells with 6S31, Doncaster to Millerhill, on 26 June 2019.

Right: Nos 254029 (43112) and 253003 (43006) are seen approaching Aberdour working 1Z43, the Edinburgh to Inverness via Aberdeen HST farewell tour, on 18 December 2019.

Below: Our jacket image No 91119 resplendent in BR Inter-City Swallow liverycrosses the Royal Border Bridge working 1S07, King's Cross to Edinburgh.

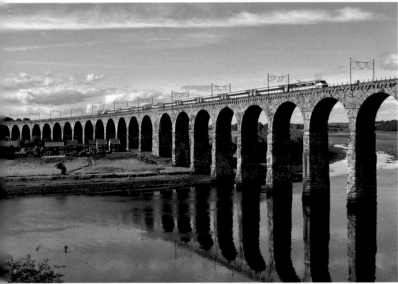

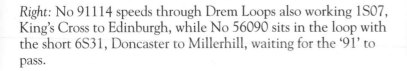

Right: No 91114 speeds through Drem Loops also working 1S07, King's Cross to Edinburgh, while No 56090 sits in the loop with the short 6S31, Doncaster to Millerhill, waiting for the '91' to pass.

David Mainor (16) Penicuik

Right: No 60163 *Tornado* leads 'The Queen of Scots' rail tour through Wester Hailes in September 2020.

Below: Maritime No 66148 is seen at Carluke with an engineering train heading towards Carlisle on 15 August 2020.

Below right: A GWR Class 158 units waits for the opposing service at Crediton.

Opposite page: An LNER 'Azuma' rounds the amazing curve at Prestonpans forming a service bound for King's Cross on 7 August 2020.

Jacob Marfleet (15)
Grimsby

My enthusiasm for trains started when I was around three, when me and my Mum would catch Class 185s, which are my favourite trains, on a regular basis. Growing up I spent a lot of time around trains and I always enjoyed seeing them.

I took my first photo of a train when I was nine. I was in Leeds and photographed a Virgin Trains Class 91 in the East Coast Trains livery. Since I

Right: A Class 802 'Nova' and Class 801 'Azuma' pass at York.

Below: A Class 68 out of service.

Below: Class 185.

Above: Class 195.

Above right: 'Voyager'.

Right: Another Class 68.

was 12 I have prioritised trying to get photos of all the different types of train around the United Kingdom. I have travelled to many lines across the country and I am always looking to try more. I regularly go trainspotting around Grimsby, Cleethorpes, Hull, Lincoln, Doncaster and York, but sometimes I will go on a special trip to somewhere different.

I really enjoy trainspotting with my best friend at the weekends. When I pick up a camera everything on my mind disappears and I am always happy. It always makes me smile when a train driver waves or gives me a tone. In the future I definitely plan to photograph different trains around the country and I'm definitely excited for the future.

I have chosen photographs of a range of passenger trains around York station taken in the spring and summer of 2021. The vibrant colours excite me, and I feel that the low floor camera angle also really helps.

Sean Mattocks (17)
Burnley

My interest in photography:Ever since I knew what a camera was I've been trying to take photos with one. They fascinated me for as long as I can remember when I first wanted to take pictures of all the trains I saw so I always knew what I had seen. From documenting my finds, my passion grew and grew as I started trying to get better pictures of both trains and other subject matter. Soon I was well and truly hooked and from 2018 onwards I've been constantly trying to better myself, pushing to improve my composition or exposures all the way to now, where I'm still just as passionate if not more to keep improving and become the best photographer I can be!

Opposite far left: No 60163 with 'The Illuminati' at Blackpool.

Opposite centre: Co-Bo restoration.

Opposite left: The people of the railway.

Right: Copy Pit climb.

Below: Whitby departure.

Below right: Lancashire local goods.

Josh McDonald (13) Malton

Right: No 47828 doubles with No D1935 on a service from Scarborough heading far west on 11 September 2021.

Below: No 20142 waits to depart from Pickering station on 13 September 2021.

Right:: The NYMR's regular 'Moorlander' train reverses through Grosmont, positioning for its journey back to Pickering on 19 September 2021.

Above: No 195115 meets No 91119's DVT at York on 16 October 2021.

Right: A TPE Class 68 turning its final corner before arriving into Malton station on an unknown date.

Louis Meddelton (18)
Christchurch

Right: Mayflower at Bournemouth.

Below: No D7612 at Ropley.

Below right: Mallard's retirement.

Ben Murray (14)
Rugby

Right: Keith signal box.

Below: 'Clag' on the Sheffield tankers.

Below right: New order, coming soon to mainland Europe.

Hugo Murray (14)
Ilkley

My photographic interests started when I regularly visited my local heritage railway. I started with rather basic shots and simple videos; however, over time I developed my skills, finding new angles and ways to make my pictures interesting. I would then often experiment with filters and effects to enhance my pieces. Since then I have continued to find new things to photograph, from landscapes to close-ups, not forgetting railways!

I find my selection of photographs interesting because they show the past in different ways, mainly seen at my local heritage railway (the Embsay & Bolton Abbey Steam Railway). I am inspired to find out how and why the railways have changed and show people all about it. The pictures show some of the different angles of the what the railways used to be like. Also, there is a brief sample of the modern railway and how it has changed compared to the old.

Top right: Industrial Hunslet *Beatrice* heads the departing 'Dales Dining' train from Embsay, while Hunslet 'Austerity' *Cumbria* rests on the coal dock after a steam test.

Below: Hudswell Clarke *Jennifer* (Works No 1731) awaits her turn in the yard at Lionheart station on the Aln Valley Railway.

Above: Another view of Hunslet 'Austerity' No 3794 *Cumbria* resting in the coal dock at Embsay after its successful steam test.

Above right: North Eastern Railway petrol-electric Autocar No 3170 at Embsay, with No D3941 and RS&H *Welsh Guardsman* (Works No 7170).

Right: LBSCR 'Terrier' No 678 (BR No 32678) *Knowle* is seen at Embsay during the Embsay & Bolton Abbey Steam Railway's 'Railway Rally' weekend.

Left: Unit No 156493 sits ready to depart as 'Pendolino' No 390008 unloads its passengers at Carlisle.

Thom O'Connor (17)
Pembroke Dock

Right: LNER Class 'A4' No 4464 *Bittern* stands in the former Hornby factory now owned by businessman Jeremy Hoskins.

Below: SECR Class 'D' 4-4-0 No 737 was built at Ashford Works in 1901, designed by Harry S. Wainwright. Withdrawn in 1956, it entered the National Collection in 1975.

A word about safety...

Our safety vision

At Network Rail, safety is paramount. Our industry is incredibly complex – our approach to safety can't be. Everyone Home Safe Every Day is Network Rail's safety promise, simple and all-encompassing.

Everyone Home Safe Every Day

We're passionate about safety, for our employees, our contractors, the passengers who travel on our network and members of the public who interact with the railway at places such as level crossings and at our stations.

We have one of the safest railways in Europe. However, serious and fatal accidents still occur. Therefore we invest in several safety awareness programmes and campaigns to make the railway a safer place for those who use it.

Railway photography and safety at our stations

Network Rail welcomes rail enthusiasts and photographers who would like to take photos or film at our stations. We'd like you to have a safe and enjoyable experience.

When you arrive at one of our stations, please let the staff at the Reception Desk know that you are there. This will keep station staff informed, so that they can go about their duties without concern about why you are there.

Act safely and sensibly at all times. Stay clear of the platform edge and stay behind the yellow lines where they are provided. We understand that in pursuit of a great image, it's easy to get distracted, so please be aware of your surroundings.

Don't trespass on the tracks or areas that are out of bounds. Don't climb on any structure or obstruct any signalling equipment or signs, which are vital to the safe running of the railway. Please don't wear anything that is similar in colour to safety clothing, such as high-visibility jackets, as this could cause confusion to drivers and other railway employees.

Flash photography is not allowed at any time. It can distract train drivers and train dispatch staff and so is potentially very dangerous. Tripods should be avoided where possible. If you need to use a tripod you must speak to our station staff to ensure you are in a safe area.

If you see anything suspicious or notice any unusual behaviour or activities, please tell a member of staff immediately. Your presence at a station or at the lineside can be very helpful to us as extra 'eyes and ears' and can have a positive security benefit. Above all, take care, be aware of your surroundings and be respectful of our passengers and employees. We want you to have a great visit and to go home safe. Our Everyone Home Safe Every Day Safety Vision applies to you too!

At the lineside

Our railway runs through some impressive landscapes and cityscapes and the images in this book showcase some of the excellent scenes that can be photographed safely from outside the railway boundary.

Please stay outside the boundary fence. You must not trespass on the railway, no matter how tempting it might be to try to secure what you think is a better image. It might be your last. Our railway is a dangerous environment, from heavy and high-speed trains, to trip hazards and risks of electrocution.

Only our employees and contractors who have been especially trained and who are authorised can be there, and rarely these days when trains are operating.

Trespass also causes significant disruption to the railway network, leading to extensive delays, cancellations and to disruption to our passengers. Trespass costs the industry millions of pounds a year. No image is worth risking your own safety, a criminal record or causing that level of disruption and cost.

Our train drivers can also be unnerved by the sight of trespassers, because they do not know what their intensions are. Trains travel at high speed and a train driver glimpsing a figure within the fence in the distance has no idea whether that person intends harm to the train or themselves. Don't be that person.

Railways make great subjects for photography. We share a passion for railways, but above all we have a passion for safety. So please take care, because we want you to go Home Safe Every Day.

Chris Gee
Operations Director
Network Rail,
North and East Route
York

Brandon Openshaw (16)
Bury St Edmunds

The reason I enjoy railway photography is that it enables me to capture the pure power and strength of locomotives. Ever since I was 13 I have been fascinated by trains and locomotives, especially steam engines, and over the years my love and passion for rail photography has become greater. Personally there is no better way to describe the happiness and passion I feel when I'm around these amazing and unique machines.

Above right: Class 37s at Norwich.

Below: Class 43 HST at Ely.

Right: Class 800s at Peterborough.

My photographs provide a good representative collection of main-line locomotives that have operated on the ex-LNER network over seven decades, from British Railways steam locomotives and diesel-electric locomotives and passenger sets to the very latest electric locomotives and passenger stock, in a variety of different liveries.

The photographs were all taken from station platforms or approach roads and therefore show how the locomotives would have typically been seen by the general public. They have been selected to show how loco liveries and station structures have evolved over the seven decades, and hence how 'the railway seen' by the general public – in terms of both rolling stock and stations – has changed under different ownerships.

Above: 'A4' 'Pacific' at Norwich.

Above right: GBRf Class 66 at Ipswich.

Right: Class 90 No 90004 *City of Chelmsford* at Norwich.

Anders Pettersson (16)
Morpeth

I am an amateur photographer living in the North East of England. I have been photographing the railway for a year or so but have been interested in railways from a young age. My local station is Widdrington, and my nearest major station is Newcastle Central. However, I enjoy travelling around the UK network taking photos of the railway in different areas. My favourite locos are heritage diesels and steam; my favourite class of diesel is Class 50 and favourite steam loco the 'A4' Class *Union of South Africa*. My camera of choice is a Canon EOS 650D with an 18-55mm lens and a 55-250mm lens.

I enjoy photographing different trains on the network from heritage to freight trains, and trialling new and different styles. My influences are from those photographers I follow on Instagram or Flickr.

My photographs span the UK network, showing a variety of locations – stations and urban areas – and train types, both freight and passenger.

Right: No 86259 *Les Ross* on the 'Cumbrian Mountain Express' sits next to Avanti's No 390129 at Carlisle.

Above: DRS No 57002 *Express* is on a route-learning duty through Middlesbrough station, passing Northern's No 156487.

Above right: GBRf No 92043 sits in the electric loco sidings at Edinburgh Waverley.

Right: GBRf No 60076 *Dunbar* operates to Lynemouth power station from Tyne Coal Terminal with biomass.

Ethan Pick (16) Ware

I have always enjoyed doing railway photography since I was very young, using my Dad's camera, but since I got my first camera for Christmas one year, I have been able to do even more photography. What I find interesting about railway photography is the different techniques I can use. I get excited from just going out and taking photographs, then showing off my photography skills on social media and trainspotting with friends.

My photos all revolve around the railway's different roles. They show passenger trains operating to holiday destinations and carrying passengers on the main line. You will also see movements such as the Railhead Treatment Train helping to make sure that the railways are safe for everyone, and trains at the end of their lives being sent to storage.

Right: A Class 313 unit enters Lewes on a service to Brighton.

Below: No 91119 passes through Welwyn Garden City on a service to London King's Cross.

Below right: Nos 66716 and 66725 pass through the Kings Meads in Ware doing their daily RHTT duties on 1 October 2021.

Above: A Class 166 leaves Dawlish forming a service to Exmouth.

Above right: A Class 57 drags a Class 465 through Welwyn North.

Right: A Class 950 and a Class 37 sit in the sidings at Welwyn Garden City.

Henry Pinkney (13) Ely

From a young age, I was taken by my Grandad for a ride in his tractor while he worked on crops in his fields. Right next to the fields was the busy freight line that connected Peterborough with Felixstowe. From then my passion for railways grew, and I watched each train go by in fascination.

2020 was quite a peak in my railway interest as there was no school due to the lockdown, so I would regularly head to my local foot crossing and video each train going by. At the end of that year I got my first camera and began photographing each train. It excited me to see how each shot turned out, and to learn more about photography.

My photographs show a range of different styles, as I like to express variety with my photos. Although restricted with my current camera, I still go on and progress in improving my photography, editing and locations. My selection shows different views of the railway by location, framing and angles; they show countryside, buildings and the general view of a railway station.

Below: DRS No 68013 (leased to Chiltern Railways) rumbles away at London Marylebone before leaving for Kidderminster.

Above: DB No 66077 *Benjamin Gimbert* GC (named after the driver killed in the 1944 Soham rail disaster) thunders through Soham working an intermodal train to Felixstowe.

Left: The Nene Valley Railway's Swedish railcar *Helga* ticks over at Wansford before tooting away for Peterborough NVR.

Above: GBRf No 66711 (leased to Aggregate Industries) applies power out of Soham with an intermodal train to Felixstowe, while a herd of cows interrupts me!

Above right: Rail Operations Group No 37800 idles at Ely Goods Loop with no driver in sight before finally taking off towards Ely Papworth Sidings.

Right: An East Midlands Railway Class 158 passes through the Fens with Ely Cathedral towering over it.

Christopher Plunkett (15) Haworth

No 78022 arrives on a rainy day.

A Class 37 in the engine yard.

A moo-ving image!
By Henry Pinkney (13)

Experimentation with adventurous new angles has always been essential to the evolution of the art of railway photography. The colours of the cows provide a dramatic contrast to the diesel-hauled train moo-ving along subtly in the distance and capture the mood of a setting sun in the English countryside at the end of another day. The photographer is a true artist and story-teller, showing us another world, right under our noses. (See page 140)

Avanti in the rain
By Shane Gopal (17)

All too often railway photographers focus on 'pretty' subjects in perfect weather conditions, portraying a rose-tinted, 'chocolate box' image of the railway. Therefore the judges were hugely impressed with this very striking picture of an Avanti West Coast 'Pendolino' battling the rain on the West Coast Main Line.

Not only has the photographer ventured out in appalling conditions to take this shot, but he has also made a feature of the rain. By capturing the raindrops and halo of spray around the train, the photographer has given this image energy and dynamism – one can truly feel the speed and power of the 'Pendolino', and the biting chill of the cold wind! It's rare that photographers put bad weather front and centre, but this photographer has done so with aplomb.

This is the railway as it is – warts and all – and defines the 'Railway Seen' theme. (See page 66)

Jack Poole (15)
Widnes

For me photography is a very interesting hobby, because I love the railway network and also enjoy sharing my thoughts on photography with other rail enthusiasts. From a young age I have been fascinated by the speed of trains and steam locomotives. I have also taken part in many things on the rail network; for example I helped out at the Welsh Highland heritage railway where me and my Grandad fixed one of the tunnels on the miniature railway line.

Photography excites me because my pictures all capture a moment in time but in different ways, encompassing one-off workings and traction, landscapes and infrastructure that won't last for ever, as well as showcasing how the railway operates to adapt to a swiftly changing.

My interpretation of 'the railway seen' is capturing what is happening on the railways currently, and how that blends in with everything from architecture and landscape as well as the rail industry itself, and how all these three things are always evolving.

These are some of my favourite shots, taken with my amazing Nikon D70s. My influence is seeing past photos that are outstanding because of their texture, colour and mood, together with the techniques the photographers have used to create the pictures.

A peacock proudly displays himself to passengers waiting for a train at Douglas railway terminus, Isle of Man, on 8 April 2019.

Right: Diesel loco *Gwydir Castle* passes the Betws-y-Coed miniature railway museum and shop on 13 February 2019.

Left: 8F No 48151, accompanied behind by 5XP 'Jubilee' No 45690 *Leander*, approaches Roman Bridge heading towards Blaenau Ffestiniog with the 'Conwy Quest' on 3 August 2019.

Below left: The station clock at Llangollen station on 16 March 2019.

Right: DRS Class 68 No 68033 waits for the 'right away' at Platform 1 at Holyhead with the return leg of a diesel special on 4 May 2019.

Below: 'A1' No 60163 *Tornado* is at Chester Reception Sidings on 11 May 2019 with 'The Mad Hatter'. The loco is waiting for a path for her to manoeuvre onto the triangle at Chester in order to turn.

Robert Pottinger (11) Romford

Above left: Day out at Darsham.

Above: A hard day's work.

Left: Diesel power.

Right: Classic AC traction.

Below: Having a break at Ipswich.

Below right: New meets old.

Adam Powell (13) Southampton

Right: No 450089 at London Waterloo with the London Eye in the background.

Below: No 313220 at Chichester.

Below right: No 37402 at Eastleigh.

Above: No 31806 at Bursledon.

Above right: No 43194 and a 'Voyager' at Bristol Temple Meads.

Right: DLR No 143 at Stratford.

Daniel Rahman (8) Chassington

For as long as I can remember I have loved trains, and I really enjoy taking photos of them so I can look back and remember all the different ones I have seen. I also like looking at photos of trains in books and magazines. My favourite photo is one I took of a train going at high speed where you can actually see it tilting.

I am a big fan of Geoff Marshall who creates train videos, through which I have learned so many facts. He has also inspired me to take my own photos and videos. I love looking at different trains and learning about them. I also love to go to stations and watch them go past at high speed; I was excited to go to Surbiton station and watch fast trains rushing by, then King's Cross station to take photos of some of my favourite trains, including the Hitachi 'Azumas'.

Right: An SWR Class 444 unit tilting slightly as it zooms past Surbiton station.

Below: A Grand Central train, and standing by the side of it the Station Manager and a cleaner talking to each other.

Above: A Hitachi 'Azuma' beside a Grand Central train at King's Cross. There is a sign on the 'Azuma' reading 'Presentation in progress. Do not dispatch', so the train had to remain at the platform.

A slow train heading for Guildford.

Daniel Ray (12) Rochdale

Northern Rail Class 142.

Class 68 TransPennine Express.

Luna Ripolles (12) London

I've always loved photography, and when you take a good photo, you feel so proud and satisfied! I love everything about it: the waiting, the watching with the camera to your eye, searching for the perfect view and sometimes just taking random photos of everything and ending up with an awesome photo by accident!

I believe that the railway is undervalued. We all take it for granted, but an incredible amount of engineering and work, as well as constant maintenance, has allowed the millions of us that use trains to carry out our daily lives.

My photographs were taken from the train window on my first journey to see my grandparents since the Covid pandemic. I photographed what most of us probably see when we take the train, but probably don't pause to really think about. In most of my photos you can also see my younger brother (unaware of my photography) looking at these things and enjoying the ride. I think having him in my photos makes them more relatable, more human, than just a train track.

My photos thus explore 'the railway seen' not only from my eyes, but also from the eyes of my brother, and my family not seen in the photos. Since the pandemic we have hardly done any railway travel, so the little things usually unnoticed sprung out at me. I'm sure this happened to everyone as they boarded their first train in months, like it does a toddler when he or she first looks out of a train, seeing the moving platform and the tracks whizzing by.

Left: Sleepy arrival.

Right: At work.

Above right: Track spotting.

Opposite top left: Graffiti walls.

Opposite bottom left: A blur.

Opposite right: Side by side.

Fergus Rostock (14) Barnstaple

I have had an interest in railways since a young age. I have fond memories of trips down to the South Devon Railway to ride the line and explore the stations, and it was perhaps these trips that ensured that my interest in railways stayed for good. My interest in railway photography developed as I took a camera to various railway locations, initially to document what I saw, but gradually I improved and began to try and compose my photographs properly. There's a lot that I enjoy in my photographs: I like the contrast of old and new as well as the atmospheric views. I try to include the main points of railway interest to convey to the viewer what is happening at that point of time. I take inspiration from the various images submitted to railway magazines and use them to improve my techniques.

In my selection I have tried to demonstrate some of the diversity of the UK's railways, included a half-and-half split between steam and diesel locomotives. I've also tried to include some contrasts of old and new where appropriate.

Above right: LMS 'Princess Coronation' Class No 6233 pulls out of Exeter St David's on a sunny September morning.

Right: A Colas Rail Class 70 and a DB EWS-liveried Class 66 are stabled adjacent to each other at Eastleigh station.

Far right: A pair of South Western Railway Class 450 DMUs coupled together at Reading station.

Above: New-build 'A1' Class No 60163 steams across the level crossing at Kingswear on the Paignton & Dartmouth Steam Railway.

Above right: The valve gear of BR 'Standard' Class 4 No 75014 *Braveheart*, resting on shed in the summer sun at Paignton on the Paignton & Dartmouth Steam Railway.

Right: BR Class 33 No 33111 in BR Blue pulls into Harman's Cross with a train from Norden bound for Swanage on the Swanage Railway.

Nathaniel Salter (17) Abingdon

I am a keen railway photographer who has grown up around trains. In 2019 I started to take photos of them and began to post them on social media and other sites. Now I thought it would be great to show off a few snaps of my journey through these last couple years.

In my selection you will find steam, diesel and classic British Rail traction. I always feel that a photograph should always have a nice backdrop, whether it being lineside with the landscape behind it or in a station with life and atmosphere providing the background.

WCR 'Black 5' No 45407 *The Lancashire Fusilier* crawls over Glenfinnan Viaduct while working the 'Jacobite' service from Mallaig to Fort William.

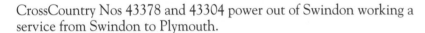

CrossCountry Nos 43378 and 43304 power out of Swindon working a service from Swindon to Plymouth.

'Avanti' No 390016 departs from London Euston bound for Glasgow Central.

Above: EMR No 43102 powers out of London St Pancras working a service to Nottingham.

Above right: LSL Nos 37668 and 37667 blast through Oxford after turning around in Hinksey Sidings while working from Bicester Depot to Crewe HS.

Right: No 7029 *Clun Castle* heads through the Oxfordshire countryside approaching Radley while working the return leg of a special from Swindon to Birmingham Snow Hill.

Max Schneider (16) Peterborough

Between studying for A-Levels I volunteer as part of the youth group at the Nene Valley Railway. Railways have been an interest since a young age, and this competition is the perfect chance to combine this with my other passion of photography. In my spare time I also enjoy painting, playing sports and going on country walks. I hope that my collection of photos portrays a diverse range of features that the current UK heritage railway scene offers. One thing I wanted to capture is the stunning and varied scenery of the British Isles, which offers a brilliant backdrop to some of the finest pieces of railway conservation in the world. Therefore, something that cannot be overstated is the importance of people to our hobby. Without the fantastic effort of thousands of volunteers and staff working for heritage railways and organisations, the legacy of historic rail travel in Britain would be all but forgotten. Overall, my aim is that my photographs don't just portray beautiful locomotives, but also the interesting architecture, wide-ranging landscape, and the work of the people that make the UK railways what they are today.

The pictures were taken using a Panasonic Lumix FZ82.

Below: Whistling curve: Tan-y-Bwlch, Ffestiniog Railway.

Light breaks through: Pickering, North Yorkshire Moors Railway.

The long way home: Northwood Halt, Severn Valley Railway.

Above: Steam, sea and sky: Weybourne, North Norfolk Railway.

Left: Passing the time: Hampton Loade, Severn Valley Railway.

Right: End of the line: Totnes, South Devon Railway.

Zahid Shah (9)
Bolton

I was inspired to become a trainspotter when I went on a train to Southport in 2016. I like taking pictures of trains because it feels to me like a reward, and it is cool to write down the number of the train. I know most of the UK's train companies and all the different classes.

What excites me about the photos I have submitted is that they are all different but have the same theme. Some of the pictures are about architecture and some are about trains and the railway, and they relate to the topic 'the railway seen' due to the fact that some feature new trains and some old trains.

Right: Yellow lights on Platform 13 at Manchester Piccadilly.

Below: Manchester Piccadilly at 8.30 in the morning.

Below right: Two symmetrical Class 185s at Hull.

Opposite main picture: The lovely roof of Liverpool Lime Street, Platforms 5 to 10. I like about the stone archway in the middle of the picture.

Opposite inset left: No 150141 heads out of Daisy Hill station – my favourite picture.

Opposite inset right: Mucky Freightliner No 37407 *Blackpool Tower*.

Zander Sheldon (15)
Sheffield

Right: Class 47.

Below: Class 60.

Below right: Flying Scotsman.

Northern Rail Class 158.

Freightliner Class 66.

Clun Castle.

Oliver Sherwood (14) Milton Keynes

This competition has been a great experience as I live in a railway town and the railway is very much part of the landscape here. I also love compositions with strong perspective lines, and railway tracks at stations are great for this. I'm not yet a professional, so I always enjoy a happy accident – capturing a moment with perfect timing feels amazing.

My submission is about the hidden art the railway gives us and how this can be unlocked by a good photograph. The pictures are how I imagine different members of my community see the railway. The three locations featured are Wolverton Viaduct, and Wolverton and Milton Keynes Central stations.

Left: The evening light provides a lovely welcome for the home-coming commuters.

Above right: Commuting without the morning rush.

Right: A unique view of Platform 3 at Milton Keynes Central station.

Far left: A rare moment capturing the curve of the railway.

Left: Weekend walkers always appreciate the view of Wolverton Viaduct, especially when a train comes past.

Below: Classic railway iconography seen from the perspective of a wet, midweek evening.

Bruno Slim (14)
St Albans

Right: No 60103 *Flying Scotsman* rests at London Paddington.

Below left: Two London Underground S Stock trains pass the light at Liverpool Street.

Below right: A Hull Trains Paragon diversion passes Elstree & Borehamwood.

Above: Thameslink No 700112 passes Alexandra Palace.

Above right: East Midlands Railway's No 222002 flies past Harpenden.

Right: London Overground No 378228 arrives at Clapham Junction.

Harry Smith (17) Leeds

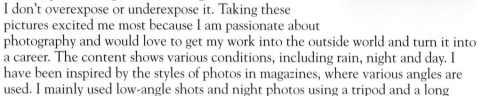

These photographs show what I am capable of making using of the knowledge gained from photography college. The modes I have used vary between 'manual' and 'sports'; manual mode is where I take a photo using manual settings to ensure that I don't overexpose or underexpose it. Taking these pictures excited me most because I am passionate about photography and would love to get my work into the outside world and turn it into a career. The content shows various conditions, including rain, night and day. I have been inspired by the styles of photos in magazines, where various angles are used. I mainly used low-angle shots and night photos using a tripod and a long shutter speed for a brighter image.

The photographs show the different kinds of trains, old and new, I have photographed over the years from TransPennine Class 68s to a Class 91 storming through Doncaster in the rain – this is my personal favourite because it contrasts the rain flying off of the pantograph as the train passes.

Above right: At 19.46 on 17 November 2019 No 67016 drags dead Nos 82202/91132 to Doncaster from Neville Hill due to the failed Class 91 on the rear. The train is 1Z46, a Leeds-King's Cross service.

Below: TPE: the old and new at York.

Below: No 91101 at York working a King's Cross-Edinburgh service.

Right: No 43285 awaits departure from Leeds to Neville Hill TM&RSD on 19 November 2019.

Bottom left: LMS 'Black 5' No 44871 *Sovereign* departs from York under a big thick cloud of smoke on 28 November 2019.

Bottom right: No 91131 passes through Doncaster on the Fast with a King's Cross-Leeds service on 17 November 2019.

Sam Smith (14) Gloucester

I have a massive passion for the railways and I have taken thousands of photographs of trains and the infrastructure around them, so it was quite a challenge to narrow the selection down to just six. The photos I selected showcase, I think, the wide diversity of the railways, and the factors that influenced my choice were varied: perfect weather and atmospheric cloud formations, with the sun in the right position; the framing of the photo to make it artistic, to capture multiple elements and the striking colours that can be seen on the railways; my positioning when taking the photographs, sometimes taken close up safely on a foot crossing or from a bridge; and incorporating the beauty of the countryside. The old and new contrast includes electric and diesel trains. Finally, I include people on the railway, capturing enthusiasts enjoying their hobby – like myself.

Above: Thank you! The current coronavirus pandemic placed alongside historic semaphore signalling.

Below: On-track checking of the infrastructure using modern technology hidden away inside a colourful, heritage train.

Below: A picture highlighting modern railway safety at a foot crossing.

Above left: A modern train pulls out of a station with some beautiful historic architecture, including a ticket office, and countryside.

Above right: Fumes from a diesel train embedded in the pollution-free electric infrastructure!

Right: Railways past and present: enthusiasts enjoying a diesel gala.

Crae Smith (14)
London

Right: London Overground No 710101 at Chingford station.

Below left: TfL No 315838 leaving Stratford station.

Below right: Thameslink No 700038 at West Hampstead Thameslink.

Photography in magazines and newspapers (1)

As many have sung, and various have claimed to have originally said, a picture is worth a thousand words … and certainly when it comes to magazines and newspapers an image can add impact to those words in a story or feature, or even *be* the visual story and carry so much of the impact.

For as long as publications have had illustrations, there has been a clamour from readers to see them, and for editors and publishers to secure and reproduce great ones … or certainly those that best support or illustrate their content.

What is the right picture?

As journalists working on Britain's leading railway magazines, our team always takes great care to find excellent pictures, which are right for what we need.

Are these always the best images? That very much depends on your point of view and what you need it for, because the first rule of journalism is always to make sure that what you are using is right for your audience, your reader, and that it illustrates the story or feature to make sure it is the best it can be.

For example, the readers of *The Railway Magazine* are very knowledgeable and appreciate new views of familiar topics.

Great railway photography tells a story, engages the reader or viewer, and is often taken from a unique viewpoint or with lighting and conditions perhaps not always considered.

But there is so much more to consider and to be aware of if you actually want to see your work in publications such as ours, or if you are wondering why we include what we do.

As a photographer you may have taken a great image, at the right time, of a great subject, and think that it should be on the front page … but is it the right shape, has it been cropped too tightly? So consider composing your image in both landscape and portrait style. A picture on a page may have plenty of sky. Why? It helps with a headline's positioning.

Is the lighting 'OK' or 'great'? For example, low winter sunlight can enhance photography and create spectacular shadows, giving a great depth to an image.

Newsworthy or artistic images?

In *The Railway Magazine* most of our images are of newsworthy events – but we do also encourage more artistic shots for our 'Portfolio' and 'Panorama' sections. In both cases, the first thing we look for is a technically competent image – is it in focus, without any motion blur, and of a useable size (which is typically an absolute minimum of 2000 x 1500 pixels)?

Above: **Crop:** Poor cropping can make all the difference… oh, this also has low depth of field, poor lighting and is of something not very rare at a location often seen. It may not make the front cover this month.

Right: **Focus:** The inclusion of foreground detail in an image such as the ash tree and sweet pea seen here can add interest, but it is important to ensure the whole frame remains in focus.

Continued on page 183

Nathan Spence (17)
Wirral

Right: Corris Railway No 7 *Tom Rolt* at Dolgoch on the Talyllyn Railway.

Below left: TR No 7 *Tom Rolt* approaches Brynglas.

Below right: No 7 *Tom Rolt* rolls off shed at Pendre.

Above: TR No 3 *Sir Haydn* in the shadows of Pendre sheds.

Right: Sir Haydn departs from Dolgoch.

Below: TR No 6 *Douglas* at Rhydyronen.

Holly Spencer (16)
High Peak

Right: In 'Cappagh Blue' livery, DCRail No 60028 slows into Peak Forest working 6Z26, the Chaddesden Sidings to Peak Forest Cemex Sidings. Seen idle in the distance is No 66434.

Below: GBRf No 60002 is seen idle on the Glossop line, just before Dinting. It is alongside the old reception sidings for the merry-go-round trains, working 6G55, Crewe Basford Hall SSM to Godley.

Right: No 802211 crawls into Platform 2 at Manchester Piccadilly at the end of working 9M26, Newcastle to Manchester Piccadilly.

Running 47 minutes late due to No 37423 *Spirit of the Lakes* suffering a flashover at Wilmslow, it was decided to send the tour to Manchester Piccadilly so that No 37422 *Victorious* could take the train onwards towards Sheffield and York. Here we see No 37422 bringing 1Z43, Crewe ETMD to York, which would later fail in the Hope Valley.

Left: Cruising into Manchester Victoria, LSL's steam loco No 34046 *Braunton* approaches Platform 4 while working 1Z52, the York to Wolverhampton 'White Rose' tour.

Right: Retro Railtours' 'Retro Cumbrian Coaster II' comes back on its return from Workington, arriving at Stockport station with Rail Operations Group's Nos 37510 *Orion*, 37800 *Cassiopeia* and 57312 working 1Z30, Workington-Chesterfield.

George Stephens (17) Darlington

I have been interested in trains for as long as I can remember. Back in 2018 I got my first camera and combined both interests. I love travelling across the UK to capture photographs of unusual and rare trains – seeing the beauty combined with the engineering really puts me in awe of what man can achieve.

I take photographs of trains in their working settings to depict genius at work, showing a contrast of old and new diesel locomotives. By doing this I can create a live work of art that can be added to over the years. As the years go by the locomotives change and new technology is introduced, and by taking photographs I can document how the railway is a living thing that will always change, evolve and grow.

ScotRail No 43035 is at the rear of an HST set departing from Edinburgh to head up into the Scottish Highlands.

Above: Nos 90006 and 90007 travel south through Oxenholme Lake District heading to Crewe Basford Hall.

Right: Nos 66848 and 66849 pass through York, with an unidentified Class 68 on the right.
Above: No 92043 at Newcastle.

Above right: No 150251 at Cardiff Central in a storm.

Right: No 56078 runs through Cardiff Central heading for Chirk.

Ben Taylor (17) Prescot

Right: No 50007 *Hercules* drags Nos 701017 and 50049 *Defiance* at Long Eaton heading to Worksop from Derby Litchurch Lane on 21 July 2021.

Below: No 66787 has just crossed Ribblehead Viaduct on a freight service from Arcow Quarry on 18 August 2021.

No 50049 *Defiance* is seen at a rain-soaked Kidderminster Town station on 15 May 2021 during that year's SVR Diesel Gala.

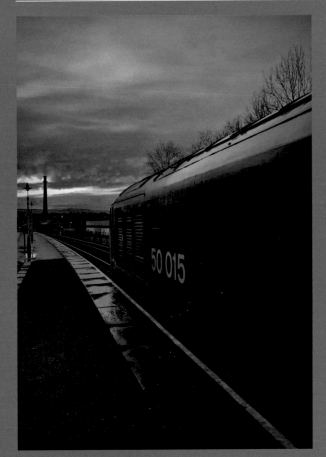

Left: No 50015 *Valiant* looks out at a lovely sunset at Rawtenstall when ready to head back to Bury Bolton Street with its final service of the day on 25 January 2020.

Right: An unidentified Newcastle Metro units passes over the River Tyne surrounded by a beautiful winter sunset on 30 November 2019.

Below: No 66164 is surrounded by an autumnal scene at Rainford Junction station as its driver gives the single-line token back to the signaller on 28 October 2020.

Hugo The Hatcher (14) Harrogate

Left: No 60103 *Flying Scotsman* approaches Thirsk with the 'Waverley' tour to Carlisle on 4 September 2016.

Right: No 86259 *Les Ross/Peter Pan* stands just outside Preston, assumed to be waiting for No 46115 *Scots Guardsman* to haul the winter 'Cumbrian Mountain Express' down from Carlisle on 8 February 2020.

Left: Nos 20305 and 20302 pass through Starbeck with the DRS 'Class 20 Farewell' rail tour to Leeds on 18 January 2020.

Right: No 91119 *Bounds Green Intercity Depot 1977-2017* prepares to depart from Doncaster with a service to Edinburgh Waverley on 1 February 2020.

Does the image work?

Beyond these basics, we look at the subject matter, the composition, the colours (or lack of) and the location. 'Does it work as an image?' we ask, meaning, 'Will it grab the reader's attention in some way?', and the more boxes it ticks in this respect, the greater the chance we will use it. A 'rare' photo of something not often seen, or in a location not often visited, will also add weight – as will the use of a location away from the classic overbridges and linesides that have been seen many times before. So choose an interesting location, research it and think of the composition; use Google Street View if it helps to find the right location.

Post processing yes or no?

We generally discourage post-processing when people ask about supplying an image for use in a magazine. It is usually far better to supply the original (beware of over-saturating and over-sharpening).

The vast majority of our readers aren't lucky enough to live in the Bahamas, and most of the time when people try to replace a sky we get a 'halo' effect. Just leave it as it was taken. If the magazine's designer requires an alteration in order to make it work on a page, we will do that in-house to our printer's specifications.

Just step back and give your subject matter breathing space, and don't digitally remove items of railway infrastructure that you think interfere with the composition. Our magazines are publications of record and show the railway as it actually is now for the benefit of future generations.

Landscape: A great landscape… taken with a medium telephoto and emphasising the autumnal colours. By not cropping too tightly the train can be a highlight.

Oh … and when you send it, if you have a high-end camera and your images are above 15MB in size, don't compress them. Send them through something like www.wetransfer.com.

Finally, and something the judges of the competition for Britain's best young railway photographer were keen to emphasise, always be safe. Gaining permission to be in locations is essential, and never put your own safety at risk.

Finally finally … enjoy it!

Tim Hartley,
Publisher
Mortons Media Group

Millie Thornely (13)
Northampton

I love gymnastics, the clarinet and photography, and have always liked capturing everyday things and scenes with my camera and my phone. I love the freedom I get from being able to try different angles and styles. I have always enjoyed photography as it allows me to express how I see the world from my point of view.

My photographs were all taken on my summer holiday trip to London; I loved travelling on the different lines and this inspired me to take my photos, applying an abstract style to two of them. I enjoyed capturing the movement of the trains and the different views I got from them as we travelled around London.

Mirror image: Kew railway bridge at dusk, seen as we walked along the Thames.

Parallel lives … parallel lines…

Social distancing.

Above: Glass divisions.

Above right: Taking a break.

Right: The diversity of the rainbow.

Harrison Tyler (13)
Oxford

I have been into trains for a long time, but the photography side has only been in the past couple of years. I'm often up and down the country on trains seeing rare movements and on rail tours. I feel that my photography has come a long way since I started and I still think it is improving as I get a better understanding of how to use the camera and where to go to get the perfect photo.

My technique is always to try and get a picture on the sunny side of the subject. I get inspired and influenced by my small group of friends; we often help and tell people what is passing and share good locations for movements.

All these pictures are of my local railway, often at my local station of Radley, which has a railway group and community offering advice and complimenting your photography. The include all types of railway activities, with steam rail tours, heritage railways, commuter trains, track testing trains, and freight moves. They all show the wide variety in the railway today, as an important part of Britain's economy.

Right: Nos 68002, 37419, 37218 and 37038.

Top right: No 43290, photographed on 1 September 2021.

Far right: Diesel gala line-up on 1 October 2021.

Above: Royal Scot,
on 6 October 2021.

Left: Class 68 set
and IET, 4 August
2021.

Right: Mayflower,
on 22 August 2021.

Owen Wade (15) Newton Abbot

Right: Industrial triple-header: Sentinel No 10077, Ruston No 429 and Class 08 No 13002 on the Plym Valley Railway.

Below: Checking tracks: Class 950 No 950001 runs through Newton Abbot.

Below right: Seaside 'Tractor': Class 37 No D6975 rumbles down Goodrington Bank on the Paignton & Dartmouth Steam Railway

Opposite page top: Class 25 No D7612 coasts through Staverton on the South Devon Railway.

Opposite page bottom left: Cambrian recreation: Nos 7822 and 7828 double-head a fish and chip special on the West Somerset Railway.

Opposite page bottom right: 'Large Prairie' No 5199 arrives at Williton on the West Somerset Railway.

Joseph Warner (18) Willenhall

My photos are a fusion of the railways of yesterday with the railways of today. I have been heavily influenced by the extensive history of the railway before me, listening to stories of my Grandad working on the early British Railways, but also travelling on the present-day railway. I used a mixture of a Canon fixed-lens camera and an android phone's camera. I also experimented for the first time by using under- and over-exposure on some of the photographs. My technique was to find as quiet a location as possible to achieve a full view of the train where possible.

The images I have selected give a snapshot of the railways today, whether main line or heritage. They were taken in 2020 and 2021 and show how the network was before potential rejuvenation, especially as the impacts of the Covid-19 pandemic will change how and when we travel for the foreseeable future. The photos show that the railways connect us to work and leisure, towns and cities, and that constant evolution is essential.

Top right: Morning at Scarborough, with a new TransPennine Express 'Nova 3' unit.

Left: 'The Moorlander' at Goathland, North Yorkshire Moors Railway.

Right: Reversing steam.

YOUNG RAILWAY PHOTOGRAPHER OF THE YEAR

19-25 portfolio: Dylan Robinson 3rd

To see Dylan's portfolio turn to page 264

Joss Webb (15) Newcastle Upon Tyne

The things that excite me most about my selection of photographs are the historical features and the variety of traction. I was also excited that I managed to get a photograph of a freight train passing Dorman Long steelworks just hours after it was demolished.

The pictures include not only a variety of traction but also historic landmarks, such as the castle keep just north of Newcastle railway station. They also feature a variety of railway jobs, such as intermodal trains and the Railhead Treatment Train.

Above left: Passing Newcastle station is No 66425 with an intermodal train to Tees Dock.

Above: No 03378 shunts the coaching stock after working a service from Percy Main during the North Tyneside Steam Railway gala.

Left: Approaching Carlisle station is a Class 390 working a service to Glasgow Central.

Above: No 68034 passes with the Railhead Treatment Train.

Above right: No 66199 passes South Bank a few hours before the demolition of Dorman Long steelworks.

Right: No 43055 is seen passing Derwentaugh working a Blue Pullman rail tour to Perth.

Nathan Webster (16)
Holmfirth

I have a huge interest in trains and enjoy capturing pictures of those I see in order to be able to look back on what I have seen and capture the memories of the good times spent trainspotting, especially with friends. The photos show trains in various locations carrying out different roles such as freight, maintenance and passenger services, demonstrating the diversity of the railways in Britain today.

Right: Two Class 20s run light through Leeds on their way to Derby. This image shows how some of Britain's oldest diesel locomotives are still operational among the modern, urban architecture of Leeds and are admired by young people and railway workers alike.

Right: The 'Staycation Express' HST is parked in the sidings at Carlisle for the night after a day of excursions on the beautiful Settle to Carlisle line.

Far right: An LNER 'Azuma' flies past on the ECML on its way to Edinburgh. This photo was captured from a safe distance at Christon Bank foot crossing.

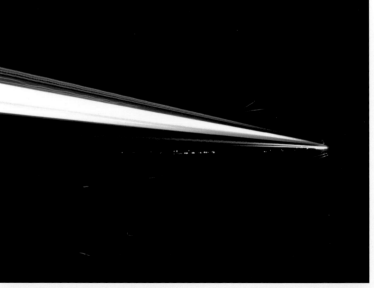

Above: Network Rail's No 950001 waits at Leeds City station to continue its vital role of maintenance and inspection of Britain's railways.

Above right: A GBRf Class 66 waits for the road at Chesterfield, being held up by another GBRf Class 66, demonstrating the importance of freight on Britain's railways.

Right: A TransPennine Express Class 397 is seen at Carlisle with a DRS Class 57 locomotive in the background. New electric trains are powering the future, but the railways are still supported by old locomotives.

Harry Wheeler (12) Nottingham

I like framing images to include something interesting as a backdrop, and I also like images taken during more extreme weather like snow. My selected photographs include very different settings; a variety of trains are pictured in a wide range of different locations, all taken in different conditions.

Right: Class 40 No 40145 pulls into Derby with a Class 20 on the rear.

Below: *The Journey Shrinker* at Nottingham.

Below right: Snowy scene: taken in January 2021, I was really impressed with the outcome of this photograph because you can clearly see the train, despite the challenging conditions.

Above: Roaring out of Rothley: a 'Deltic' prepares to depart.

Above right: No 66731 takes the Sleaford avoiding line in dull conditions.

Right: A 'Warship' tackles Eardington Bank. This picture was taken in May and I wanted to make sure to get the beautiful scenery in the background. I am really proud of this image because you can see the dandelions on the embankment below the train.

Nathaniel Whiffen (16)
Barry

Above: A pair of Transport for Wales Class 175s await departure from Swansea.

Above right: GWR No 43094 stands at Cardiff Central after terminating from Penzance.

Right: GWR No 43185 waits at Swansea on the last day of long-distance operations.

Right: Now 20 years old, 'Voyager 20' No 220016 stands at Bristol Parkway awaiting departure to Plymouth.

Below: No 166221 stands at Severn Beach waiting to depart for Bristol Temple Meads.

Below right: No 50007 stands at Bristol Temple Meads waiting to depart with the 'Mazey Day Cornishman' rail tour.

Mckenzi Whincup (13) Epsom

I have autism and ADHD and my passion in life is trains. I prefer diesel trains to steam trains and electric multiple units (EMUs). It is my ambition to gain employment as a train driver with a freight train company. I have also sent many letters to different train companies and received letters and items back; I even received caps from Canadian National Railways, which are proudly displayed in my games room at home and form part of my collection. I am very safety aware around stations and crossings, and when I'm not in school I am usually out and about riding trains or visiting railway events.

I am very fond of diesel locomotives, and am glad that some have been preserved, allowing myself and other train enthusiasts to still be able to ride behind them. My overall favourite diesel locomotive is the Class 66, but I didn't manage to capture a photograph of one in time to submit.

I used my iPhone on a tripod to capture the images I have submitted, and all were taken on the Epping & Ongar heritage railway.

Alex Widdowson (18) Burgess Hill

Railway photography has always interested me, allowing me to capture so many unique and special shots in different railway locations for future use and enjoyment. There is always a good feeling when you look back through your camera roll or SD card and find something that creates that unique scene.

With some people it's all about the precision, but that's not often the case with me. I just shoot was seems right at the time, whether it's the location, light, atmosphere or simply because I can. This can be seen in the pictures I have provided, whether its the river location, the light of the sunset or the atmosphere of the steam.

The pictures include a variety of locations, rolling stock, light and atmosphere, from a far-away view to a close-up or an 'it's all about the background' – no two railway photos are the same, as my selection demonstrates.

Above right: An SR 'Q' Class approaches Bewdley on a September evening in 2019.

Left: 'Manor' No 7802 and 'Hall' No 6990 leave Quorn & Woodhouse with the sun rising over a cold Leicestershire morning.

Right: No 31101 follows the River Dart in July 2019.
Above: No 41313 stands at Wootton at the Isle of Wight Steam Railway in June 2019.

Above right: SR 'S15' No 847 makes a smoky and steamy departure from Sheffield Park in January 2020 (taken with a Personal Track Safety Certificate).

Right: No 4414 approaches Bewdley Tunnel with the sun setting in September 2019. *Above:* Settle.

Ben Wigfall (12) Wirral

Below: Preservation.

Right: Castle bypass.

To see Liam's portfolio turn to page 216

Ben Wilkinson (14) Southam

I first became fascinated with maps when I was in nursery; this quickly led to me to discover the map of the London Underground and from there my love of trains grew. I found out as much as I could about Underground trains, visiting the depot at Acton and going on trips around the system. As I have grown older I have studied railway track diagrams and found out about the variety of trains that run on the UK network.

During the Covid-19 lockdown in spring 2020 I started to take photos of trains on my local railway using my mobile phone. This has quickly grown into frequent visits to not only the local line but also further afield to see a wider variety of locomotives. I am now using my Dad's old bridge camera, which has enabled me to take more detailed and better-quality photos. I enjoy taking pictures of rare and unusual trains such as special-liveried locomotives and rail tours. I am looking to further develop my photography skills and discover new techniques to improve my pictures. I

now pay more attention to things like lighting and atmosphere, as well as looking for different and unusual angles to capture unique images.

The competition theme made me think of what the everyday person sees but usually takes no notice of. I wanted to make the unseen seen by capturing images of the working railway, documenting the railways of today in a time of great change.

Opposite page top: Screaming through the sunshine.

Opposite page far left: Full steam ahead.

Opposite page left: Unsung hero.

Above: TeamRed.

Above right: Powering the nation.

Right: Early morning electric.

Aidan Wilson (16) South Shields

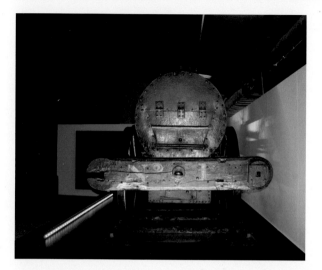

Left: In the beginning.

Right: Hurricane Thompson.

Below: Farewell 125.

Part 2: entrants aged 19 to 25

We now arrive at the second age group featuring the work of photographers between the ages of 19 and 25. There were a total of 41 eligible entrants in this category. Once again the diversity and range of coverage were impressive. As with the images in Part 1 the photographic equipment used varied considerably from phone cameras to high-end SLRs and DSLRs. We were particularly pleased to find that photographic film was also in evidence. Enjoy!

Image by Lewis Hurley (see page 244)

Christopher Ainscough (24) Wigan

My fascination with photography started in May 2010. Back then I was more into film, and would constantly go venturing across the country with a video camera and a tripod to film steam engines, then upload them to YouTube.

I went to college in 2013 to study Media, which is when I slowly started transitioning to photography and got myself a Canon 700D. After three years at college, I ended up studying Film Production at the University of Central Lancashire in Preston, and it's at this point I really got into railway photography, although I was more focused on film.

I love looking back at how my skills have changed and love the photos I take now. My selected images are some of my proudest captures and I look forward to getting even better in the future. They were taken at the right place, at the right time. I love the morning and evening lighting, and included are some of my favourite photos taken during various photo charters and night shoots.

The pictures examine the theme by looking into how the railways used to work back in the era of steam. The cameo shots I have taken really help to tell how the railways were run, whether it be shunting wagons around the yard or getting an engine prepped for service; they just give off a sense of what it must have been like.

Above: L&YR Aspinall Class 23 tank No 51456 passes Burrs Country Park with the sun beginning to set, photographed during a 3p20 short freight photo charter on 26 February 2020.

Right: The fireman of Sentinel No 7232 *Ann* and the shunter watch on while Manchester Ship Canal No 4002 *Arundel Castle* shunts some box vans around the yard during the same photo charter.

Left: Basking in the sun: Black 5 No 44871 passing Townsend Fold signal box

Right: Sentinel No 7232 *Ann* shunts a couple wagons around Bury Transport Museum, seen during a 3p20 photo charter on 10 September 2021.

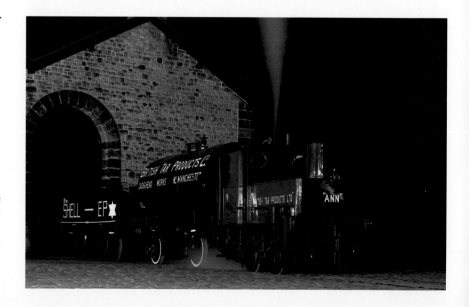

Top right: LNER 'A4' No 60009 *Union of South Africa* has it's 'cod mouth' open on Baron Street shed. The photo was taken during 3p20's 'North Eastern' night shoot on 2 September 2021.

Right: After a long day, a footplate crew member refills the sandboxes of No 60009 while on shed during the same night shoot.

Timothy Amor (24) Melton Mowbray

Recording what's in front of me with regards to railways has always been very important throughout my life. What you see today may not be there tomorrow. Posterity is the name of the game. When you have that shot, you have history in your hands, and that's what drives me to do what I do. Even when I'm long gone, my pictures will be there for future generations to enjoy and to reflect on how far the railway has come.

This photographs relate to the set theme as they covers the three main types of traction currently in use, both on the main line and in preservation, showcasing railway and rolling stock developments over the decades.

Below: A 'Pendolino' pokes out of Birmingham New Street on the last day of Virgin Trains.

Below right: A beautiful 'Black 5' approaching Quorn & Woodhouse on the GCR.

Above right: An LNER HST on the ECML arrives at Grantham station for the very last time on 21 December 2019. The set was painted in its original 'Inter-City 125' livery, a paint scheme many people adore.

Opposite top left: A CrossCountry 'Turbostar' passes Brooksby AHB Crossing, Leicestershire. The slow shutter speed puts the emphasis on speed.

Opposite top right: An 'Azuma' in bokeh with the 'Have you closed the gates?' sign in focus at Frinkley Lane bridleway crossing, north of Grantham.

Opposite right: GBRf No 66762 passes through Melton Mowbray in wintery conditions.

Matthew Anderson (23) Skipton

Right: Cumbria storms past Draughton with Queen Victoria's saloon.

Below right: Hudswell Clarke No 1208 sits warming on Embsay shed.

Below: Cumbria runs around its train at Embsay.

Above: No 18 *Jessie* awaits the road to depart.

Above right: Beatrice trundles along the iron road.

Right: Norman sits at Bow Bridge in the fading daylight.

Liam Barnes (20) Rossendale

Railways have been in my blood from a very young age, having first visited my local line of the East Lancashire Railway at the age of three. Now aged 20, I've been incredibly fortunate enough to not only volunteer, but also begin on the career ladder with the railway that started the passion in the first place, as an engineering apprentice at the ELR's Baron Street loco works.

My first interest in photography also came from the ELR, attending an Autumn Steam Gala in 2014 with a small compact camera. This was a brand-new aspect to my interest that I had not explored before, and I quickly became fixated by it, constantly wanting to learn more. Over the last few years, as my camera equipment has grown, my taste has also developed and simply through self-teaching and taking inspiration from some pioneering photographers such as the great Ivo Peters I strive to portray a different perspective in railway photography from the standard 'front three-quarter shot'. Through my photographs I very much wish to keep the image alive in terms of our heritage – it's something that means a great deal to me, and I believe it is vitally important to educate the younger generation so that they are able to see railway scenes of the past, today.

Ivo Peters once said, 'For me, one of the greatest pleasures of railway photography has been when I have discovered some enchanting new location, and then set about trying to get the most attractive picture of the scene.' This very much resonates with the style of photography that I've tried to develop, always searching for that composition that little, or nobody, has ever done before.

Above: 'Time's up.' Now retired, No 60009 *Union of South Africa* sits in Ramsbottom station as the late-shift porter checks his watch on a dark December evening (self-portrait).

The competition theme immediately made me question just how I perceive our railways in the 21st century. The answer was that, despite living in a modern world, it is still entirely possible to recreate authentic scenes of our rich and vibrant railway heritage.

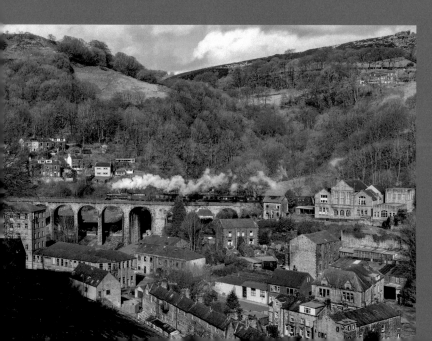

Right: Mirrored inside Mytholmes Tunnel on the Keighley & Worth Valley Railway, 4F No 43924 powers through the portal.

Left: Weaving through cotton mill towns, 'Jubilee' No 45699 *Galatea*, disguised as
218
219
No 45562 *Alberta*, crosses

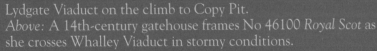

Lydgate Viaduct on the climb to Copy Pit.
Above: A 14th-century gatehouse frames No 46100 *Royal Scot* as she crosses Whalley Viaduct in stormy conditions.

Above right: Racing through the night, No 34046 *Braunton* heads through Walsden in the Calder Valley.

Right: A dramatic display in torrential rain as No 46115 *Scots Guardsman* negotiates the cutting towards Stainforth on the Settle & Carlisle Railway.

Anders Beavis Berry (19) Tewkesbury

Railways were the main catalyst for my interest in photography and are still the main thing I photograph. I like the endless variety and scope for creativeness that railways bring, as well as the excuse to travel and explore new places. It is also possible to photograph other things that you wouldn't necessarily otherwise see, for example an unusual flower behind a rural station platform, or breathtaking landscapes visible through the train window.

An interesting photographic view can be found in most places, be it an urban area, countryside or run-down former industrial wasteland. I enjoy taking pictures in these (and other) settings. The presence of a railway is an added bonus, but not essential; there are plenty of other things to focus on, such as architecture or nature. However, in my view the best pictures combine all these features. I believe the images reflect the diversity of the modern railway scene, presented in a creative way. I have taken inspiration from the environment surrounding the railway to frame each photograph. I really like the contrast between the images, both in their type (for example long-exposure, landscape, architecture) and content (Scottish Highlands, London skyscrapers, farmland).

These pictures show the railway in the summer of 2021, all over the country.

Below: Flying Scotsman heads south near Fiddington, Gloucestershire, with a London-bound rail tour.

Above: No 66765 rests at Paddington on the rear of the 2021 GBRf charity rail tour, as a GWR IET departs for the West Country.

Opposite: Nos 377616 and 377454 await their next workings at London Bridge, with The Shard looming tall in the background.

Opposite top right: Nos 50007/049 bask in the sunrise at Gloucester, having just been attached to a Penzance-bound rail tour.

Below: Nos 37407/425 double-head the return leg of Day 3 of the 2021 GBRf charity rail tour across the headwaters of Loch Awe near Dalmally.

Below: A watch-mechanism statue and old wrought-iron pavement feature.

John Liam Blundell (24) Liverpool

I've always loved railway photography, trying my best to get that top-class image. This selection features a mixture of old and up-to-date trains.

Right: Two Class 40s pass through Winsford.

Below: A ScotRail Class 170 passes through North Queensferry as the rain rolls in.

Below right: West Coast Railway Company Class 47s, working a rare rail tour on the Merseyrail Northern Line, pass No 508138.

Above: No 66731 *Captain Tom Moore* at Huyton.

Above right: No 60163 *Tornado* is seen at Roby with the 'Ticket To Ride' rail tour.

Right: Brand-new Merseyrail unit No 777010 is at Formby with a test run service.

Ruth Briselden (25)
Sidcup

A trip to the Ouse Valley Viaduct with my drone.

No 51456 at Burrs
By Chris Ainscough (24)

'The judges were impressed by the initial dramatic impact of the picture and the good use the photographer has made of the flooded area of the foreground field. The exposure used has meant that good detail is retained in the colourful sky and the reflection in the water has added interest to what would otherwise have been a dark area of the picture. (See page 210)

Reflections of the Tyne & Wear Metro
By Maude Webster (20)

When I first saw this image it immediately jumped out at me. I love the minimalist aesthetic, but it still manages to tell a story. The composition is perfect, the gentle distortion of the reflection of the bridge in the water, and the blue hues are very pleasing. The addition of the moon adds context and brings to mind an early-morning commute to work. (See page 284)

Jack Clarke (22) Spalding

I'm a young railway photographer with a wide range of interests in the subject matter. I have been interested in railways since I was young and was taken to see the steam trains at Nene Valley or the big main-line tours through the Peterborough area.

In more recent years I've got into photography and have spent plenty of time in different parts of the country to visit spots on the main line or on heritage lines to photograph anything from an 'A1X' 'Terrier' doing brake van rides in Wansford Yard or a 'Deltic' roaring down the East Coast Main Line.

For me railway photography gives me a reason to get out and travel, to see completely different areas with more varied rosters. What excites me about my selected photos is a variety of subjects, a mix of classic steam engines and more modern diesel traction.

Above: 'Deltic' No 55019 *Royal Highland Fusiliers* roars into action on a cold damp evening for the Nene Valley's 'Jolly Fisherman' train.

Left: The North Norfolk Railway is also known as the 'Poppy Line', and here War Department No 90775 is seen entering Weybourne station with a cluster of poppies in the field nearby.

Below: The legendary *Flying Scotsman* steams gracefully over the impressive Harringworth Viaduct, the longest in the UK.

No 35018 *British India Line* runs past the signal box at Whittlesea station during a memorial charter for the late founder of the Railway Touring Company, Nigel Dobbing. This was a rare sight for the region.

Two Colas Class 56s are out on the March to Peterborough line in a more rural area.

Freightliner No 66414 is seen just past Whittlesea station with the staggering 2,000-plus tonnes of Network Rail's most impressive train, the High Output Ballast Cleaner, with Heavy Haul Class 66s managing this mighty load.

Eliza Coulson (22) Glasgow

My six images hope to celebrate the rich history of railways here in the Highlands of Scotland, from the 100-year-old architecture of Glenfinnan Viaduct to ScotRail's modern service train to Strathspey Steam Railway based in Aviemore, and the dedicated team of men and women who care for the railway's small fleet of heritage engines.

Experiencing a rail journey today can feel as though one is following journeys travelled by many people before, through buildings and infrastructure that carry a history. The railways of Britain are a true testament to resilience and resistance, which we can still feel today as we continue to fight for our vital lifelines, particularly those linking big cities and remote country areas.

In my images I try and capture a different perspective of railways, perhaps a side we do not get to see in our busy lives. Using my 35mm analogue camera I aim to create this reflective view of this section of our railway.

Two spectators wait to capture the train crossing Glenfinnan Viaduct in November 2019.

Strathspey Railway crew, fireman and driver, in August 2020.

Far left: Smokebox door, August 2020.

Left: In the shed, Strathspey Railway, July 2020.

Below far left: A Strathspey Railway steam engine ready to go for the day shift in Aviemore in July 2020.

Below: A ScotRail journey through the valley in November 2019

Ben Cox (21) Milton Keynes

I started DSLR photography five years ago, using a Nikon D3300, and have been a keen photographer ever since, capturing not only railway scenes around the country but also military aviation from various RAF bases. I am now looking to upgrade my camera to improve my photography quality and continue to practice and improve my skills.

What excites me about my photographic selection is the sheer range of motive power that even in the 21st century is still available to see and photograph on a regular basis. This is emphasised in my submitted pictures by modern electric multiple units, old BR diesel multiple units and pre-BR steam locomotives. I have attempted to show different styles and ways of capturing these trains at work; in an era where everything is standardised, there is still a great variety to be seen on the UK's railways.

I have tried to take inspiration from the railway photographers of yesteryear, who recorded not only special scenes but also the normal services of their time. As we all know, the railway scene is ever-changing, and something that may be commonplace today may be all but gone tomorrow!

Opposite left: The sight of LNER 'B1' No 61306 *Mayflower* brightens the otherwise gloomy landscape near Banbury, hauling a Steam Dreams express to Stratford-upon-Avon on 22 August 2021.

Opposite bottom left: Avanti West Coast 'Pendolino' No 390137 speeds northwards through Leighton Buzzard with a service from Euston on 7 March 2021.

Opposite bottom right: The old order: in its unique purple EMR livery and with less than a month left in service, No 43274 flies north near Bedford on 29 May 2021.

Right: A time for reflection: LNER 'A4' No 60009 *Union Of South Africa* simmers in Wolverton Works on 23 November 2019 after limping in the night before with a hot axle box.

Below: No 46100 *Royal Scot* makes for a fine sight approaching Kings Sutton with a train for Salisbury on 4 September 2021.

Below right: The claret coaches of the Royal Train reflect the last few rays of the day's sun while passing through Linslade on their way to meet the Queen at Euston on 27 June 2019.

Matt Dawe (23) Cardiff

This selection of pictures represents the evolution of my photography style, which stemmed from the purchase of my first 'proper' camera in 2018. The photos represent the joy I find in taking photos from new or different angles, as well as the experimentation I have been trying over the last few years, trying to take photos that aren't simply 'three-quarter profile' portraits (although I still take a fair few of them as well!).

Growing up I was an avid reader of *The Railway Magazine* and always loved the 'Panorama' sections and others that showcased amazing railway photography. I have long been trying to replicate the quality and style of these amazing photos. This selection also demonstrates the many ways in which the railway is seen. All represent modern facets of railway operation, which influence how they are seen today.

Left: The unveiling event for new-build GWR No 2999 *Lady of Legend* at Didcot. Here the loco is on the Didcot turntable during the 2019 'Hall & Saint' gala on 8 June.

Right: Three generations of narrow-gauge motive power on the Welshpool & Llanfair Light Railway on 28 July 2021. No 823 *Countess*, diesel No 17 and No 7 *Chatterden* rest in Llanfair Caereinion yard. I was working at the railway at the time and photographed this during a celebration for the anniversary of No 822 *The Earl* returning to Welshpool. The shot was obtained with appropriate safety training and I was in the presence of a number of other senior members of staff during a closed event.

Right: R&ER *River Esk* is framed by an abandoned motorcycle at the former stone-crushing plant at Murthwaite Quarry while heading a Dalegarth-bound train on 2 July 2021. I spent the day hiking from Eskdale to Ravenglass and was pleasantly surprised to find that a public footpath ran through the former Murthwaite site, allowing this shot to be taken.

Below: Another enthusiast observes Hunslet 'Austerity' 'WD' No 198 *Royal Engineer* running round at Wootton on the Isle of Wight Steam Railway on 24 September 2020.

Above: Lady of Legend at work on Didcot Railway Centre's 'main line'.

Right: Photographers record the arrival of *Lady of Legend* at Eynsham station, Didcot Railway Centre, during the 2019 'Hall & Saint' gala.

Kristian Faulkner (24) Huddersfield

I had always been interested in photography, but it was at college that I really started to explore it and it was there that I really gained an appreciation for the darkroom. I felt that only having a finite number of frames made me work harder to take better pictures. When I left college I became a graphic designer and didn't Take more than a few images for probably three years.

Then the pandemic hit, and by the second major lockdown I was really starting to feel the 'cabin fever', so for some reason one day I picked up my camera and fell in love again!

I became interested in railways when I was very young. I think it was something about the size and scale of the locomotives, but also the way the network was structured, combined with countless trips to the NRM.

I think the images I've submitted are interesting because I have tried to juxtapose the new with the old, and to show the evolution of our railway network, with some aspects of it maybe only five years old, and some maybe 50 or even 150, yet all of them working in unison. I've tried to photograph the obvious parts of the railway that people see, but position them among other aspects of the railway that people might not realise is or was part of it.

Right: A TransPennine Express Class 185 unit on the line between Deighton station and Bradley Junction.

Below left: A Northern Class 158 unit passes the former Bradley station at Bradley Junction near Huddersfield.

Below: BR No 27001 operating on the Keighley & Worth Valley heritage railway.

Below: A Grand Central Class 180 passes a Northern Class 158 unit on the line between Brighouse and Halifax.

Above: An LNER Class 800 on Arthington Viaduct.

Right: No 60163 *Tornado*, operated by WCR, passes Ribblehead station.

Cody Froggatt (21) Deeside

Nine to five grind.

Above: The future is in safe hands.

Below: Lost to time.

Above: Day dream.

Below: Track check.

Above: Whistling through Chester.

Aidan Glenister (24) London

I bought my first camera, a 40-year-old Canon AE-1, in 2020 as a lockdown hobby and have been shooting with film ever since. Time with my camera is hard to come by these days as I'm currently training at the Military Academy, Sandhurst. One of the pictures I've submitted is a special one for me because it was the first good photo I took after buying my camera, at Earl's Court Station one morning on my to work at my old job!

.

Below: Station.

Above: Westbound

Below: Square indeed.

Louis Graham (23) Northallerton

Right: 'A4' 'Pacific' No 60009 *Union of South Africa* on the 'Bon Accord' charter from London King's Cross to Edinburgh Waverley.

Below: LNER HST No 43314 on a service from Aberdeen to London King's Cross, seen from Platform 1 at Darlington Bank Top station.

Bottom right: A brand-new LNER Class 800 'Azuma' on it first run from Leeds to London King's Cross is seen at Wakefield Westgate.

James Griffiths (19) Hull

I work for Northern Trains, and my pictures are intended to capture the true vision of British engineering, and represent the engineering heritage we have in the UK. The inspiration behind them is Ivo Peters's work on the Somerset & Dorset Joint Railway, which showed the engines at various stages of their careers, and this is what I wanted to achieve here.

My photographs show how the combination of heritage and modern infrastructure and trains can be seen today. They represent a combination of style, age and evolution of the railway, including heritage railways, main-line steam and diesel, and one of the newest locomotives in the UK.

Right: 'A1' No 60163 *Tornado* accelerates past its railway ancestors at Grosmont on 23 September 2021.

Below: Isambard Kingdom Brunel's roof at Paddington, seen on 1 July 2021.

Left: No 45407 accelerates out of Fort William with the 'Jacobite' on 6 June 2021.

Opposite top: No 67010 passes along the causeway at Conwy in North Wales on 4 May 2021.

Right: Nos 48305 and 5428 *Eric Treacy* thunder up the incline out of Grosmont on 23 September 2021, passing No 2999 *Lady of Legend* and No 825.

Far right: No 60163 *Tornado* accelerates out of Hull Paragon on 30 September 2021, the first steam engine to visit the station since 2002.

Luke Hamilton (21) Darlington

I have been enthusiastic about trains for my entire life, beginning with Thomas the Tank Engine. However, I only started my photographic hobby at the end of 2016 when I moved to Darlington College (which is, of course, situated right next to the East Coast Main Line). I also joined the Stockton & Darlington Railway Youth Team based at Bishop Auckland, which is when my hobby took off.

Every day after finishing college I'd walk to Darlington station and stand on the platforms for about two hours, which gained me my first friends on the railway. In 2019 I made an unexpected return to the youth team by volunteering at one of their adopted stations at Darlington North Road; I currently look after the plants there during warm weather as well as making regular trips to ensure that the station is kept tidy and any faults are reported. I also volunteer at the Head of Steam Railway Museum in Darlington.

These photographs were taken in the last couple years around the railway network and show steam and diesel locomotives as well as DMUs. Featuring old infrastructure and new trains, they show scenes of Britain's railways old and new.

Above: Despite not being operational, Worksop East signal box still stands proudly opposite the town's station, and has been a Grade II listed building since 1986. No 195004 heads away from Worksop with the 14.54 Sheffield to Lincoln service on 27 August 2021.

Left: On the scenic seawall between Dawlish and Teignmouth, GWR No 43010 leads a 'Castle Class' set on the approach to Teignmouth with No 43022 at the rear. The train is the 08.00 Cardiff Central to Penzance service on 7 September 2021.

Opposite top left: As the sun sets on a glorious summer's day, Northern No 156444 stands at Eaglescliffe with a Saltburn to Darlington service on 6 June 2019.

Opposite top right: Formerly owned by Direct Rail Services and now owned by the Harry Needle Railroad Company, No 37612, on hire to Colas Railfreight, leads the 08.52 Derby RTC to Selby Barlby Loops Test Train through Worksop on 23 August 2021, with No 37057 trailing at the rear.

Right: West Coast Railways No 33029 leads No 31128 into Church Fenton in the setting sun on the return journey of the final 'Scarborough Spa Express' of 2021 from Scarborough to Carnforth on 16 September.

Jake Hardiman (22) Wallingford

My selected photographs represent the sheer variety of traction available to photograph and travel behind on the UK network. I like to focus not just on photographing the train but the picture as a whole, paying close attention to aspects like lighting and composition, to produce the best possible pictures.

My photography depicts almost every facet of the wider UK railway scene as a whole, featuring diesel- and electric-powered passenger and freight services, as well as heritage steam railways and main-line diesel rail tours. The pictures also emphasise the inspiring architecture of the UK's stations, which can be equally impressive whether old buildings like York or newer ones like Reading.

The fact that what we see on the railway today is so diverse in terms of age is a testament to the country's various preservation movements, and I hope that this diversity can continue for many years to come.

Right: A GWR Class 800 IET at sunset at Reading.

Below: GWR 'Prairie' No 4144 at Damems Loop on the Keighley & Worth Valley Railway.

Below right: Colas Rail No 56090 at York on a working from Doncaster to Whitby.

Daniel Holbrook (25)
Sunderland

Right: Whillan Beck in the sun at Dalegarth.

Below: Whillan Beck approaches Miteside.

Below right: Whillan Beck and *The Bug* at Fisherground.

Lewis Hurley (21)
Coventry

Iaim to provide a message or story behind each photograph I take, and locations are chosen specifically for that reason. As a result, I invest a lot of time and effort into travelling and researching new places. Exceptions include locations such as Tyseley and Shilton, which I have been visiting for a number of years since I was a child. In these instances, I always seek to try something different, and explore new angles to set my images apart from other railway photographers.

My selection explores perspectives such as time periods, surroundings/environment, and perceptions of the railway. I believe it's important to explore the theme from different perspectives, rather than one, which is why I have included photos that convey messages of environmentalism, heritage and retro, and the eyes of railway enthusiasts.

Above right: GBRf No 66788 *Locomotion 15* hauls 4L18, Trafford Park-Felixstowe North, past the giant wind turbines at Daventry. The turbines and trees in the background help to give an environmental theme, whilst the intermodal train shows how railfreight is more environmentally friendly than going by road.

Above: No 86259/E3137 *Les Ross/Peter Pan* flies through Dordon, Warwickshire, with 1Z86, the London Euston-Carlisle 'Cumbrian Mountain Express'. This picture shows how it is possible to get authentic-looking photos in the 21st century – there's very little to suggest that this is a 2021 photo besides a few locomotive details!

Left: A blend of the old and the new: No 43102 *The Journey Shrinker: 148.5mph – The World's Fastest Diesel Train* in retro Intercity livery passes Leicester forming a Nottingham-London St Pancras service as it would have done in the 1990s. The Class 47s, 56s and 58s on the depot also help towards this '90s theme, while the track layout and Mk3 livery reminds us that it is the present day.

Above: Colas Rail's No 37175 on the rear of 1Q98, the Cambridge to Cambridge via Norwich and the Wherry Lines Network Rail test train, passes the boarded-up Lakenheath signal box, showing the irony of on-track maintenance passing an old structure that has been left to decay.

Above right: 'Castle' Class No 7029 *Clun Castle* slows into Tyseley with 1T51, the Stratford-upon-Avon-Birmingham Snow Hill 'Shakespeare Express'. The GWR architecture and station features make the locomotive look 'at home'.

Right: No 37425 *Sir Robert McAlpine/ Concrete Bob* gleams in its Regional Railways livery as it is reflected in the Oxford Canal at Shilton, working 0Z68, the Daventry IRFT-Crewe Gresty Bridge. The use of natural features, such as the canal or water in general, can create interesting imagery.

Frankie Hutchings (24) Shrewsbury

I feel that my selected photographs show the past and future of the railway, with pictures of steam locomotives and dated infrastructure as well as the more modern railway with its large new infrastructure; the picture of Wembley shows the increasing level of freight that will be transported on the railway.

My main interest in taking railway photographs is to capture the speed, scale and movement of the steam locomotive, captured here in various modes of operation, from the engines at rest at Didcot shed to the 'Black 5' working hard on the climb leaving Shrewsbury.

All the photographs were either taken from a vantage point that is accessible by foot or from within a railway carriage itself. These are the two most common ways for people to see the railway, myself included. Additionally the various forms of motive power depicted in the pictures help to show how the railway has been seen by the public and will continue to be seen into the future with more modern forms of motive power.

Right: A view from inside Didcot locomotive shed on a public open day, 21 July 2019.

Below: A private steam charter leaves Shrewsbury and heads for Craven Arms on 2 April 2021.

Opposite top left: A different perspective of passing Wembley, seen from a train window (a Euston to Shrewsbury service on 13 August 2021).

Opposite top right: In the Castlefield area of Manchester on 29 September 2021, a passing service train heads to Deansgate station with the Beetham Tower in the background.

Right: A public foot crossing on the Severn Valley Railway, slightly north of Highley station, photographed on 18 September 2021

Far right: No 60003 *Flying Scotsman* heads towards Staines station on a charter train on 1 June 2019. The picture was taken from a multi-storey car park overlooking the railway.

Dafydd Keen (19) Llandeilo

What really excites me is when I see some locomotives that I have never seen before, so much so that I cannot help but take a photo of them, whether during a trip to a heritage railway or on a local line.

This selection of photographs documents my meetings with trains. I think it is fun to photograph engines from different angles, and taken together these pictures represent the railway viewed through my own lens and represent my own personal view of the railway – how I see it.

Right: Work in progress, on the Gwili Railway.

Below: No 45321 *Sherwood Forester* has failed at Llandeilo and is waiting in a siding to be taken away.

Below right: A view from my home railway, the Heart of Wales Line. This is Swansea station, where many trains meet.

Right: Sherwood Forester is seen at Carmarthen before it failed, surrounded by photographers, fans and children.

Below: Our little local train crosses a bridge over a public footpath.

Below right: Double 'Pacers' on the Llanelli & Mynydd Mawr Railway.

Chris Kirton (21) Leicester

I first started to photograph trains from the age of 10, having picked up my interest in railways from a very young age at the Nene Valley Railway. I always enjoy photographing trains, specially at my local heritage line, the Great Central Railway, as well as steam and classic traction on the main line.

I enjoy the variety of trains on the National Network, but also heritage railways, and just point my camera at anything railway-related.

Above: No 48624 steaming past Kinchley Lane, GCR.

Left: Evening 'Azuma' arrival at Peterborough.

Left: Nottingham HSTs.

Opposite left: Class 20 reflection.

Opposite top right: BR Blue and Green DMUs meet at Rothley, GCR.

Opposite bottom right: Old and new Great Western meet at Didcot.

Andrew Lamport (23) Ely

I was relativity new to the photography scene when these images were taken, inspired by my father's records of the railway during his adolescence. I had missed much before I took up amateur photography, so spent these years trying to record as much as possible before I missed my chance.

This collection of images summarises my early years of railway photography, my passions and how I documented them through the lens. A lot has changed since I recorded these scenes and experiences, so they're now important memories.

Above right: 'Wherry Line' 'Tractor', 2 July 2019.

Right: 'Castle' on the Cotswold banks, 8 May 2019.

Below: Bongo heading for the Broads, 31 August 2019.

Right: The freedom of travelling and reuniting with loved ones had been lost for a long period throughout 2020 and the beginning of 2021. I captured this scene in York station after the Coronavirus lockdown had been relaxed.

Far right: Having taken over from the Class 20s that had dominated the Railhead Treatment Trains throughout North and South Yorkshire for many years, Class 37s were booked on the RHTTs during the 2020 season. On 9 November 2020 No 37402 in BR Large Logo livery is seen storming out of the fog and darkness through Driffield en route to Bridlington before turning back and heading to York later in the evening.

Bradley's portfolio features on this and the following two pages

Bradley Langton (20)
Driffield

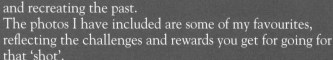

I am a keen railway photographer with an ambition to capture the ever-changing scenes on the railway, in a style that represents myself and my photography. My main focal interest is steam, and recreating the past. The photos I have included are some of my favourites, reflecting the challenges and rewards you get for going for that 'shot'.

I always try to be different, taking shots that I feel can be seen as inspirational not only for myself but for my audience. I enjoy taking photos in challenging conditions and proving that rewards are achievable. All these pictures show today's railway scene, with visions of steam and attempts to recreate the past, combining them in a present-day scene. I have also included day-to-day scenes, some of which we have learned to cherish more than others.

Right: A pool of water on Platform 1 at London King's Cross on 1 June 2021 provided an opportunity for this reflection of one of LNER's Intercity 225 sets. A few sets had recently been brought out of retirement to assist with the shortage of Class 800/801 'Azuma' trains.

Opposite bottom left: The sights and sounds of steam under the canopy of York station are something that will always be enjoyed and cherished. No 45562 *Alberta* (actually No 45699 *Galatea*) is seen wheel-slipping on 24 June 2021 while taking the last portion of the 'Scarborough Spa Express' through to Scarborough, having just taken over from a pair of Class 37s that had brought the tour from Carnforth.

B.LANGTON PHOTOGRAPHY

Right: BR 'Black 5' No 45212 crosses the ever-popular Glenfinnan Viaduct on 8 September 2020 with the 14.15 'Jacobite' service from Fort William to Mallaig in typical Scottish weather, showing the difficulties in trying to photograph during these poor conditions but also displaying the atmosphere that can be achieved.

Below right: The distinctive shape of a Merseyrail Class 508 is seen as it is lit up by another member of the class before they cross paths in the tunnels under the Mersey with services to and from Liverpool. They are seen from Hamilton Square station on 10 August 2021.

Joshua Monks (19) Helston

I grew up in Cornwall and have always been interested in railways and railway photography. In 2017 I joined the Helston Railway as a volunteer, then in late 2020 moved to South Yorkshire as a student at the National College for Advance Transport & Infrastructure; this move brought me closer to railway lines and gave me a chance to take more photos.

These photos show how the UK rail network can be seen in a day-to-day setting; they also show the typical rolling stock to be found, from freight to commuter rail to high-speed rail. I enjoy taking photos, as they provide a snapshot of an industry at one moment in time – I am photographing history. I like to photograph both the rolling stock and the infrastructure, such as station buildings and bridges.

Right: An unidentified Avanti West Coast Class 390 races through Rugeley Trent Valley station forming a service from the North to London Euston.

Below: Transport for Wales Class 158 No 158883 arrives at Shrewsbury station as an Aberystwyth to Birmingham International service in August 2021.

Above: Colas Rail Class 70 No 70809 passes through Barnetby in July 2021.

Top right: DB Cargo Class 60 No 60020 departs from Swinton (South Yorkshire) station with a Toton to Doncaster move.

Right: Sheffield SuperTram No 111 passes the Sheffield Canal near Attercliffe tram stop.

Left: West Midlands Trains Class 172 No 172333 arrives at Stratford-upon-Avon station forming a service from Kidderminster.

Thomas Poole (19)
Lancaster

Right: With the upland areas of the Lake District dominating the background, Nos 68034 and 68007 power over Galgate working 4M27, the 05.46 Mossend to Daventry, on 21 October 2021. Usually worked by an electric Class 88, due to recent high electricity prices this diagram was substituted for diesel traction for a short period.

Below: Nos 57002 and 57003 pass through Prestwick Town working 7Z98, the 15.24 Kilmarnock Barclay Sidings to Crewe Basford Hall, on 10 August 2021. Despite being completely the wrong time of year for snowplough movements, they had just been released from overhaul at Kilmarnock.

Below right: Nos 43031 and 43146 make a stop at Dunkeld & Birnam working 1H51, the 12.08 Glasgow Queen Street to Inverness service, on 12 June 2021. There have been talks of relocating the station to enable the duelling of the adjacent A9; also, the station has poor accessibility for boarding and alighting passengers, which is another strong argument in favour of the rebuilding.

Above left: Nos 508123 and 508138 accelerate away from Freshfield towards Woodvale RAF base working 2S01, the 06.16 Hunts Cross to Southport service, on 20 July 2021. Time is running out for the Merseyrail 'PEP' units, which are due to be replaced by the new Stadler Class 777s. No 508123 is also one of the four Merseyrail units to carry a 'face mask' vinyl at the cab ends, encouraging passengers to wear a face covering as a result of the Covid-19 pandemic.

Above right: No 37510 powers through Bolton-le-Sands with a defective No 397005 in tow working 5Q08, the 12.23 Manchester Longsight to Kilmarnock Long Lyes, on 19 October 2021.

Right: No 158717 climbs through the Strath of Kildonan and approaches the tiny (and little-used) halt of Kildonan itself working 2H57, the 14.00 Inverness to Wick service, on 14 July 2021.

Daniel Powers (21) Tunbridge Wells

I'm currently studying Mechanical Engineering at Southampton University, and have had a passion for the railways since a very young age. Once finished with university, it is my dream to work on the rolling stock used across Britain's railways. I have enjoyed growing up through a time of great innovation on the railways and am excited by new stock.

I really got into trainspotting in my mid-teens and only a couple of years ago I got my first DSLR. Nowadays I consider myself a wildlife and landscape photographer first, and rail enthusiast second. However, these pictures show opportunities taken to capture a variety of scenery and stock across the country. I am constantly looking out for special trains and unique locomotive movements, to remind me that the railway is more than EMUs and DMUs for commuting. Using my DSLR has helped a lot in bringing out creativity in my railway photography.

In some of these images I have tried to capture what the railway means to people and the joy it brings them. I have also included one of men working on the railway, as they are often forgotten. Others demonstrate my creative side, trying to place the trains as aesthetically as possible, and including references to their past, present, and future in the scene.

All these images were taken from station platforms, so these are all sights that are easily achieved by the average commuter, but not necessarily appreciated.

Left: The man in charge.

Above: Patience.

Below: Passing the torch.

Right: The ancient industry.

Opposite top right: Centre of attention.

Opposite bottom right: In all weathers.

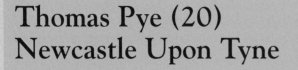

Thomas Pye (20)
Newcastle Upon Tyne

Below: GBRf No 66733 *Cambridge PSB* passes Blea Moor signal box near Ribblehead heading to Clitheroe with a Castle Cement train on 10 July 2019.

Opposite top left: Nos 37419 *Carl Haviland 1954-2012* and 37409 *Lord* Hinton at Carlisle on 30 September 2019.

Opposite top right: Nos 37219 *Jonty Jarvis* and 37521 at Durham on 1 November 2019.

Opposite bottom left: No 43311 crosses Wetheral Viaduct while working a diverted LNER service to Edinburgh Waverley on 22 September, 2019.

Opposite bottom right: New-build 'A1' 'Pacific' No 60163 *Tornado* is seen at Prudhoe on 1 March 2019.

Dylan Robinson (19) Cradley Heath

My interest in the railway has always been with me since I was a toddler, and I can only blame my Grandad for that! I began photography with my Mum's Lumix compact camera, not having a clue how to get a 'good' photo of a train. A few years later I had been using my iPod Generation 5 to take photos and videos of trains wherever I went, then one day my Grandad purchased a new DSLR, and let me use his Canon 300D.

Something that motivated me was taking to social media to publish my images, little knowing how much the younger generation enjoyed the railways as much as I did. I began to get a following and enjoyed the satisfaction of people enjoying my photos and giving constructive feedback.

I now hold two qualifications in photography that I took in college, and have also won a competition in college, my objective being to advertise their safety campaign in an eye-catching manner. After entering college I had gained a whole new sense of freedom and began travelling more up and down the country. I have included in my selected photographs both modern and vintage traction to show the different aspects and environments they create.

In the future I aspire to continue with my railway photography and to keep improving, visit new places and meet more new people. I find the hobby enjoyable and it allows me to be unapologetically myself!

Right: A 'Santa Special' on the Avon Valley Railway.

Top right: No 68009 pauses at Birmingham Snow Hill.

Bottom right: No 68027 stands at a rather miserable York station bound for Scarborough on 20 December 2019.

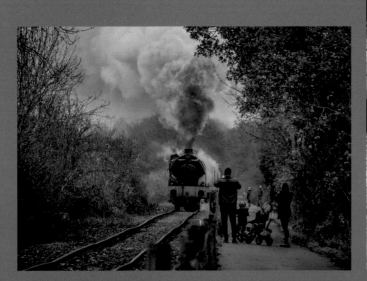

Above: 'Stop. Look. Listen. Beware of Trains' – a scene at Water Orton foot crossing on 14 April 2018.

Top right: No 66040 works a Parkandillack to Exeter Riverside train running 21 minutes early as it passes Cockwood beside the Exe estuary on 24 April 2019.

Right: No 172007 has just arrived at Leamington Spa from Nuneaton as Nos 37610 and 37612 prepare to depart after the driver changed ends on 5 November 2019.

Andrew Rothe (25) Sheringham

I have been a rail enthusiast from a very young age, but my serious interest in photography really started during my undergraduate years while I was attending university in Nottingham. I was studying for a BA in Creative Media and, inspired by my tutor Danny (whom I credit with teaching me almost everything I know about photography), I experimented and branched out with different pieces of equipment. I consider every day out with a camera to be a learning day.

Having recently finished a Masters degree in Museum & Heritage Development at NTU, I look forward to not only continuing my photography as a hobby but also bringing my work into a professional and museological context through future projects in the heritage sector.

I'm inspired by the work of railway photographers like O. Winston Link, Robin Coombes and Les Nixon, and thoroughly enjoy seeing their work. In my work I select the themes and people that constitute the railways of Britain in the 21st century. I always seek to capture a blend of traditional compositions as well as more 'outside-the-box' ideas.

I've included a range of photos from across the UK, and have tried to include a wide variety of subjects and settings. Each of the chosen shots shows a different way in which the railway, or a part of it, is seen by different people – a what is seen is as important as what isn't seen.

Below: Great Longstone for Ashford station closed in 1968, but this Grade II-listed structure still sees plenty of visitors passing through the platforms, such as on this October day in 2020. These days, however, they're walkers and cyclists making their way along this former Midland railway trackbed that now forms part of the picturesque Monsal Trail.

Above: Looking like a man out of time, a steam locomotive driver checks his watch as he confers with the crew of a First Great Western HST on a drizzly day in Cornwall in July 2019. Only 34 years stand between the build dates of the Austerity 0-6-0 steam locomotive he's been driving and the Class 43 HST power car.

Above: Some more rural railways are hard to access. This stretch, located in the Cambridgeshire Fens near the town of Whittlesey, is an incredibly remote location. A GBRf Class 66 hauls a container train in August 2021, photographed from the back of a small motor boat on the river that weaves around the railway line in this region.

Above: At York station in early March 2020 a trinity of tractive power can be seen by the crowds amassing on the platforms and congregating outside the perimeter fencing. An electric Class 91 leads an LNER passenger service into a platform, a diesel-electric CrossCountry Class 220/221 'Voyager' departs heading north, and 70-year-old BR 'Standard' No 70000 *Britannia* sits with a recently arrived rail tour on the right.

Right: 'A1' 'Pacific' No 60163 *Tornado* crosses Ribblehead Viaduct in October 2021. This looks like a quintessentially British railway scene from any time in the past 40-50 years, but 50 years ago there were no Peppercorn 'A1s' left, and 40 years ago this now-iconic Settle to Carlisle line was under the very real threat of closure. So while this scene may look timeless, it's actually very much a scene from the 21st century.

Left: Those who volunteer or work on heritage railway see different things as compared with passengers. Here, Met-Camm DMU No M51188 sits outside the sheds of the North Norfolk Railway's Carriage & Wagon Department in April 2019, fresh from overhaul. The vehicle and its pretty rural backdrop are framed by the yellowy lighting and less aesthetically pleasing interior of the workshop.

Matt Slack (20) Ripley

Right: One company, three liveries.

Opposite page top left: No 43299 on its third job is as many years passes a former EMR colleague.

Opposite page top right: The early bird catches the worm.

Opposite page bottom: A newly 'aubergined' Class 222 'Meridian' motors over the River Soar.

Below: An ex-LNER-liveried EMR HST flies under George Stephenson's Grade II-listed Mackney Road bridge.

Below right: Fifty shades of green.

Bradley Slater (24) Alnwick

My photographs document the new LNER 'Azuma' and TransPennine 'Nova 1' trains going through a range of different local stations, as well as showing the old architecture at these locations. I was influenced by the recent developments in train design and wanted to showcase them.

My selection explores how modern trains can blend in with old stations, so I aimed to emphasise the concept of old meeting new.

Right: An LNER 'Azuma' speeds through Chathill station on Friday 29 October 2021.

Opposite page top left and top right: LNER 'Azumas' pass through Acklington station on Monday 25 October 2021.

Opposite page bottom: A TransPennine 'Nova 1' at Chathill station on Friday 29th October 2021.

Below left: An LNER 'Azuma' heads south through Morpeth station on Tuesday 26 October 2021.

Below right: A TransPennine 'Nova 1' is seen at Morpeth on the same day.

Edward Smith (19) Marlborough

Right: Colas Railfreight Nos 66846 and 66850 haul the daily Railhead Treatment Train past Purton in Swindon.

Below: No 43004 brings up the rear of a Cardiff-bound service under the iconic roof of Bristol Temple Meads.

Below right: Nos DR98976, 166213 and a Class 455 unit on the blocks at Reading.

Opposite page top left: No 66533 pauses on the Up Main at Swindon.

Opposite page top right: No 60163 *Tornado* at Newbury on its way to Taunton.

Opposite page bottom: LSL's 'Midland Pullman' stands at Plymouth working a charter service from Eastleigh to Penzance.

Matthew Smith (23) Wrexham

I am currently in my first year at Rose Bruford College studying for a BA(Hons) Lighting Design. I have been a theatre lighting technician for three years and an amateur photographer for six. I've always had an interest in railways, which has developed rapidly through the years. My interest in photography began in 2012 during the Ffestiniog & Welsh Highland Railway's 'Kids Training Week', using my Dad's old Olympus Stylus 400. That Christmas I got a Nikon Coolpix L810, then eventually in 2015 I received a Canon EOS 700d, which I still use to this day.

I find photography a way of relaxing, especially after a tough week of work. There are days when I have a lot of photos but none I am happy with, and other days when I have a good selection, but I always enjoy it regardless of the weather or the outcome. I enjoy going out and seeing what the day brings and the challenge it brings along with it. One of my favourite things about a photograph is that it is a captured moment in time and gives us something to look at in the future, to enjoy or think about.

My selected photos were taken while out and about exploring, taking in my surroundings, planning, and playing with my camera. They show a mix of traction on the main line today, old and new.

Below left: Three DRS BR Large logo Class 37s with two TSOs and a BSO pass through Stafford on a move from Norwich to Crewe on 7 January 2020.

Below right: Silence before the storm: it's 06.30 on a cold Friday morning at Wrexham General, a couple of hours before the rush to work on 31 January 2020.

Opposite page top left: LNER 'A4' No 60009 *Union of South Africa* approaches Wrexham General's Platform 2 passing a Virgin Trains Class 221 'Voyager' that has just arrived from London Euston on 17 September 2019.

Opposite page top right: Phones out: BR 'Standard' No 70000 *Britannia* is greeted by onlookers and passengers boarding the train as it arrives at Crewe's Platform 6 with a private charter on 30 March 2019.

Opposite page bottom left: LMS 'Black 5' No 45231 *Sherwood Forester* passes Croes Newydd North Fork, Wrexham, on a test run on 6 February 20. In the days of steam Croes Newydd engine shed was on the left of the image, and there was a small rail yard on the right until around the late 1980s/early '90s.

Opposite page bottom right: Fast off: an Avanti Class 390 departs from Crewe's Platform 6 for Liverpool Lime Street during the evening of 31 January 2020.

Nathaniel Smith
(20) Loughborough

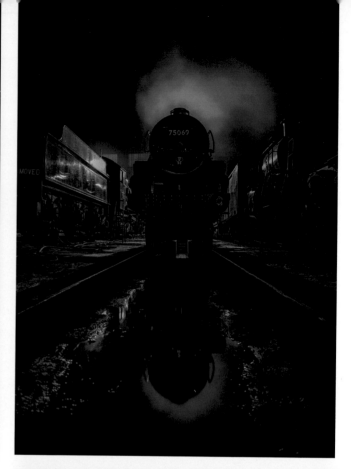

Right: Standard Bonfire Night.

Below: Raining in Leicestershire.

Top right: A Star is born again.

Below right: Heavy metal.

RAILWAY MUSEUM

The National Railway Museum's 'Vision 2025'

Supporting the Young Railway Photographer of the Year 2022 comes at a pivotal moment for the National Railway Museum. At a time when audiences are changing, we feel the need to speak to and reflect young people in our stories and exhibitions. We couldn't be prouder of celebrating the work of young photographers of the railway with this inaugural competition.

Telling new and different stories of railways, past, present and future, is the cornerstone of our masterplan. Vision 2025 is our six-year journey to become a global engineering powerhouse and a reinvented, inspiring 21st-century attraction, and will transform the National Railway Museum, York, and Locomotion in Shildon.

Our transformed museums will show the cutting-edge innovations shaping our world today—alongside the extraordinary birth and growth of the railways. By celebrating the past, present and future of railways and engineering, we will capture the hearts and minds of the next generation of engineers, innovators and thinkers.

Vision 2025 consists of a series of projects. Central Hall, our new entrance building, will sit at the heart of the redesigned National Railway Museum site, the gateway to our transformed museum. Wonderlab, an interactive gallery primarily (but not exclusively) for 7-14 year olds, will be a ground-breaking interactive gallery exploring the how, what and why that underpin the creation of the railways. The green backbone to the museum's development, South Yard will provide our community with open space to picnic and play.

At Locomotion, a brand-new building will house impressive displays and draw on Shildon's unique heritage as the cradle of the railways. This sustainable open store will create opportunities for visitors to engage with the museum's collection and be an inviting presence that emphasises Locomotion's pivotal role as a cultural cornerstone for the community.

To find out more and to support our work, visit railwaymuseum.org.uk/2025 or contact Julie Moody, Campaign Director (julie.moody@railwaymuseum.org.uk)

Above right: Artist's impression of the new Central Hall from Museum Square. Credit: Feilden Fowles Architects.

Right: Artist's impression of the new collections building at Locomotion. Credit: AOC Architects.

William Smith (19) Otley

My interest in photography really took hold in around 2017, when I finally had a phone capable of taking photos to a reasonable standard. Simultaneously, my deep-rooted interest in railways and particularly in steam also began to develop. By December 2020 I had moved to Lancaster University and my phone wasn't able to handle

Above right: Signalman and fireman carry out the token exchange at Damems loop. Ivatt 2MT No 41241 is passing Fowler 4F No 43294 with its mixed rake of Mk1 stock and Lancashire & Yorkshire six-wheelers.

Below: Stanier 'Black 5' No 45212 rests at Haworth yard on 16 December 2020, having just arrived from Carnforth for the winter period.

the requirements of the setting and the West Coast Main Line, so that Christmas I treated myself to a Nikon D3500 with both the 18-55 and 70-300 lenses. I instantly regretted not buying it sooner!

My selected photos represent the first three weeks of my ownership of the camera. Soon afterwards the ability to go out and take railway photos was hindered by the national lockdown. During this time I started spending more and more time out in the landscape and my interests in photography developed away from just railways towards wildlife, landscape and sunset photography.

My photos are now at a point where I'm usually quite pleased with what I return home with. Photography has also allowed me to make new connections and is responsible for my getting involved in heritage as a volunteer at the Embsay & Bolton Abbey Steam Railway.

The photographs cover some very different landscapes, whether open countryside in the valleys, on shed or in a station. They show the diversity of the railway scene, with different elements of architecture and heritage structures displayed together with a mix of human and physical elements.

Bottom left: No 41241 runs round the 'Elf Express' at Keighley station on 19 December 2020. This loco stands out from a great many in preservation thanks to its vibrant livery, also visible is Keighley's historic railway architecture cornered in by more modern structures such as the local Asda.

Above right: Class 37 No 37294 passes the top end of Stoneacre Loop on the Embsay & Bolton Abbey Steam Railway on 12 December 2020. This working formed part of the line's 'Santa Specials' through the scenic Yorkshire landscape.

Right: No 41241 makes a spirited departure from Oxenhope station in the snow on 29 December 2020. The powerful exhaust paired with the steam heat leaks makes for quite an atmospheric shot.

Brendan Thorburn (22)
South Queensferry

Right: No 45690 *Leander* passes Dalmeny on a Scottish Railway Preservation Society special.

Below: No 60009 *Union of South Africa* passes Dalmeny.

Below right: No 46512 at Grantown-on-Spey.

From Railways to Royalty by Jack Boskett

Photography is a superb medium for telling a story, explaining an event or describing a point in history. All of this is certainly true in the railway industry, and one photographer who currently excels in making the most of an 'alternative viewpoint' is **Jack Boskett**. Marking an accolade of 12 years as a professional photographer in 2022, today his work is widely recognised in railway publications and literature for various Train Operating Companies and heritage railways.

Jack carries a wealth of experience, which has led him to work with Prime Ministers, Secretaries of State and members of the Royal Family. Jack has had a camera in his hand since the age of five and won a photographic competition at the Gloucestershire Warwickshire Railway in the under-18 category in 1997, when he was at the tender age of seven. His father, an avid amateur photographer, took him out to photograph steam engines around the country from an early age. He used to set up the camera and give guidance as to when Jack should press the shutter, together with tips about composing the image. The rule of only taking one photograph to save film was drummed in from the start, as slide film was expensive, and this precedent is something that Jack still uses today when he uses his digital.

Jack didn't study photography at college or university. His skills developed over time, with years of practice, correcting mistakes and learning from them, which enabled him to push his love of photography further. While still at school he had his first picture published by Chris Milner from *The Railway Magazine* in 2005. It was after this that he caught the bug to photograph trains for railway publications and continues to do so to this day.

Combining railways and photography, he began his journey as a professional photographer in 2010 at the age of 19 during the depths of a recession. Like many other photographers, he began his career specialising in wedding, portrait and commercial subjects. This was to test the water and to find his feet in the big wide world of the photographic industry. It wasn't long before he realised that he was a very small fish in a big pond! Two years in, he found that his niche of railways opened doors to other industries as time passed.

Today, Jack's work is widely recognised in a plethora of industries and also the national press. Having made several television appearances and performances on the stage, he tours the country 'treading the boards' with his one-man stand-up photography show 'From Railways to Royalty'.

Jack is an advocate of today's railway photography, and many of his images will go down in history. He always endeavours to help the younger generation to follow in his footsteps and progress in the way he did from an early age. He cannot wait to see the results from the Young Railway Photographer Awards and wishes all the entrants every success in the future.

Horsepower! A 19-year-old cob horse named Shandy gallops alongside Southern Railway 'Merchant Navy' Class No 35006 *Peninsular & Oriental Line SN Co* at Didbrook on the Gloucestershire Warwickshire Steam Railway on 22 September 2021. It took three years to plan and carry out this scene with the 10.00 Toddington-Cheltenham Race Course service. With a once-in-a-lifetime moment, there was an enormous amount of pressure for the horse-rider, and Jack had to ensure that the timing was perfect as the two subjects passed the camera in unison.

Her Majesty the Queen unveils her name at London Paddington on the side of a Great Western Railway Intercity Express Train on 13 June 2017

Toby Way (24) Bracknell

Photography for me is honestly just something fun to do. I just enjoy taking photos when visiting railways and trying to capture a moment or scene to remember for years to come. Memories may fade but sometimes a picture can be worth a thousand words.

Above right: Spirited departure.

Bottom left: Sunset 'Scotsman'.

Bottom right: 'Where are the chips?'

Opposite page top left: 'Teddy Bear' shuttles.

Opposite page top right: Slumbering giant.

Opposite page bottom: Pride of the line.

Maud Webster (20)
Newcastle Upon Tyne

I am currently studying for an Architecture & Urbanism degree, and I especially find fascinating the ways that the railway industry impacts the built environment and has shaped the lives of so many people and the spaces in so many cities. I enjoyed curating this series of images, and considering the space generated with the railways that remains absent without trains.

I feel my work adheres to the theme strongly as it considers the actual tactile, present visual nature of trains.

Above left, right and below left: Pullman experience.

Right: Speed limit!

Right: Reflections of the Tyne
(& Wear Metro)

Above: Toy village: the Royal
Border bridge at Berwick.

Harry Wykes (19) Malvern

Below: Transport for Wales's No 158825 has just crossed the 1860s Barmouth Viaduct, working a Cambrian Coast passenger service from Machynlleth to Pwllheli on a cloudy day during August 2021.

Bottom: No 7714 approaches Bewdley station on the Severn Valley Railway, shortly after passing Bewdley South signal box, working on a goods train during the autumn gala in September 2021.

Above: Great Western Railway unit No 158951 approaches the snow-covered Malvern Hills during January 2021.

Opposite top left: Avanti West Coast No 390115 passes through Rugby during a storm on 28 July 2021.

Opposite top right: New West Midlands Railway unit No 196101 arrives at Worcester Shrub Hill on a test run from Tyseley LMD, passing under the 1970s signal bracket on 17 May 2021.

Right: Network Rail Class 97s leaving the town behind shortly after crossing Barmouth Viaduct while operating a rail charter from Pwllheli to Bristol on Friday 20 August 2021.

Network Rail owns, operates and develops Britain's railway infrastructure: that's 20,000 miles of track, 30,000 bridges, tunnels and viaducts, and thousands of signals, level crossings and stations. We run 20 of Britain's largest stations while all the others, more than 2,500, are run by the country's train operating companies.

Usually, there are almost five million journeys made in Britain and more than 600 freight trains run on the network. People depend on Britain's railway for their daily commute, to visit friends and loved ones and to get them home safe every day. Our role is to deliver a safe and reliable railway, so we carefully manage and deliver thousands of projects every year that form part of the multi-billion-pound Railway Upgrade Plan, to grow and expand the nation's railway network to respond to the tremendous growth and demand the railway has experienced – a doubling of passenger journeys over the past 20 years.

Jessops believes 'Image is Everything' and we love to help our customers tell their stories through photography and video.

We pride ourselves in guaranteeing to our customers unrivalled expert advice together with access to the highest quality digital imaging and photography equipment, accessories and services, fulfilling the needs of hobbyists all the way through to professionals.

Jessops also offers a full range of digital print and personal gifting products and solutions both online and in-store to ensure that our customers make the most of their images and creativity. Having invested in our own Jessops Academy Training Team, we promote education and creativity at all ages across the digital imaging space.

The National Railway Museum in York is home to iconic locomotives and an unrivalled collection of engineering brilliance, celebrating the past, present and future of innovation on the railways. As part of the Science Museum Group, we are dedicated to igniting our visitors' curiosity about the people, places and engineering marvels behind the railways.

Silver Link is a renowned rail, maritime, road transport and biography publisher. Recently acquired by Mortons Books and incorporating the imprints Past and Present and The Nostalgia Collection, Silver Link offers a wide range of titles aimed at the enthusiast and nostalgia markets.

The name Mortons may not be familiar, but the magazines we publish should be known by many if not all rail enthusiasts across the UK and even around the globe.

We are Britain's leading publisher of rail titles, including *Heritage Railway*, *Rail Express*, *Railways Illustrated*, *Steam Days* and, of course, the record-breaking and class-leading *The Railway Magazine*, which this year celebrates its 125th anniversary and is still leading the way as the nation's best-selling publication on this topic we all love. With railways just as relevant today as they were in the late 19th century, our stable of titles will have your passion covered, and we have been delighted to play an active part in this brilliant competition.

Bauer Media UK reaches over 25 million UK consumers through a portfolio of world-class, multi-platform media and entertainment brands.

Steam Railway is one of Britain's leading heritage rail titles, and has been at the forefront of the railway preservation scene for more than 40 years. *Steam Railway* focuses entirely on steam – no diesels or electrics here. Written by enthusiasts for enthusiasts, with incisive news, comment and analysis on the world of railway preservation – coupled with lively topical and archive articles – *Steam Railway* is the magazine of choice for fans of heritage steam. *RAIL* is the leading bi-weekly magazine for Britain's modern railway scene. Written by some of the industry's most respected writers and commentators and published every two weeks, *RAIL* is up-to-date and gets to the heart of the issues affecting Britain's railways, whether it is incoming rolling stock and motive power, or new government legislation.

The Bahamas Locomotive Society, a registered charity, is one of the very few voluntary groups owning and operating a steam locomotive on the main line. No 45596 *Bahamas* was restored between 2013 and 2018 with the assistance of many thousands of individual contributors to the National Lottery Heritage Fund, and is based at Ingrow on the Keighley & Worth Valley Railway, where the BLS has its headquarters, workshop and an accredited museum.

For further details see www.bahamas45596.co.uk.